CRAZY FAITH

JACK EASON
AND FRIENDS

SHADOWROCK PUBLISHING

PRAISE FOR CRAZY FAITH

PRAISE FOR *CRAZY FAITH*

Crazy Faith is an inspiring collection of stories about ordinary people, from both the Bible and Jack's personal experience, who exhibit infectious faith in an extraordinary God.

- Aaron Shust
Centricity Recording Artist/Songwriter

Jack Eason is passionate about connecting people to their ultimate purpose—finding and following God's plan. This practical book will inspire you and challenge you to take the risks to follow God's plan for your life. When you do, you embark on the great adventure of discovering life worth living. Read this book and get moving!

- Dr. Jeff Lorg
President, Golden Gate Seminary; Author of
The Character of Leadership and *The Painful Side of Leadership*

Many are deeply driven to clearly hear the voice of God within their own hearts. *Crazy Faith* not only provides biblical principles for the discernment of God's voice in our daily lives, but gives tangible examples of how many serving in the kingdom today have heard and are hearing God's voice in their daily work. In the era of the Christian-celebrity, it is insightful to read a book that focuses its attention upon true servants who are making a kingdom impact without being on camera. *Crazy Faith* will be informative and inspiring to all who pick it up.

CRAZY FAITH
STORIES FROM
THEN AND NOW

Jack Eason and
Friends

Crazy Faith: Stories from Then and Now

by Jack Eason and Friends

Published by Shadowrock Publishing

2607 Woodruff Rd. Suite E #418

Simpsonville, SC 29681

ISBN 978-0-692-51306-4

Copyright © 2015, 2018 by Jack Eason

Cover design by Adam Hall, atomcreative.net

For more information on this book and the author, visit: www.crazyfaithbook.com

Unless otherwise noted, Scripture quotations are taken from THE HOLY BIBLE NEW INTERNATIONAL VERSION® NIV ® Copyright © 1973, 1978, 1984 by International Bible Society. Used by permission of Zondervan Publishing House. All rights reserved.

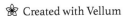 Created with Vellum

Library of Congress Cataloging-in-Publication Data

Eason, Jack and Friends

Crazy Faith: Stories from Then and Now / Jack Eason and Friends

Printed in the United States of America

❀ Created with Vellum

Dedicated to my Family and my small group,
the ones who inspire me to live by
CRAZY FAITH.

CONTENTS

FOREWORD

As a Christian, I'd like to think I have a strong faith in God. After all, I've read so many stories in the Bible where God did amazing things in the lives of those that truly chased after Him. But for some reason, I still have days where I question God. Where is He? What is He doing? Why won't He answer my prayer?

It's usually in moments of desperation that I find myself on my knees, pleading with God to show up. To give direction. To bring comfort. To help me. And then He does ... usually in unexpected ways.

As a filmmaker, I've had plenty of ups and downs. But the more I learn to walk with God, the more I expect those days where He allows me to be "stretched" in my faith. You see, that's when I do the most growing. Unfortunately, I don't grow much when things are smooth and comfortable. In truth, I tend to get lazy and apathetic if I stay in a quiet season for too long. But I've found that as a child of God, He doesn't let me stay there. He challenges me, tests me, and calls me to a deeper level of faith and obedience.

That's when I'm put in a situation where "safe" faith is not enough. To make it through the fear, uncertainty, and sense of failure, I have to get a little crazy with my faith. I have to remind myself that I follow the God of creation, who made the rules in the first place. I have to put my trust in the Word of God that says He can do the impossible. I have to believe that He loves me and wants to glorify Himself in my life. And I have to do this, even when my logic tells me to run away.

When I look back at the MANY times God has out-performed, overcome, and overwhelmed me with His power and faithfulness, I find myself wondering why I ever question Him in the first place. But that's easy on the backside of a crisis. It's on the front side or during a trial that you have to get a little crazy with your faith. But I'm here to say that it's worth it. Every prayer, every confession of sin, every hope, and every tear.

God wants to know you intimately. He wants to show Himself strong in your life. But to do that, He occasionally allows an obstacle course for your faith. So the next time you find yourself facing something that's bigger, scarier, and more uncomfortable than what you think you can handle, get on your knees and turn to God. Let Him know that you need Him, and that you believe He can get you through this mine field. Then determine to cling to His Word and to obey whatever He tells you to do ... even if it's a little crazy. Because He is on the throne and in control!

May God Be Glorified!

Alex Kendrick,
Producer/Director of WAR ROOM, FIREPROOF, COURAGEOUS,
FACING THE GIANTS

1

GOTTA HAVE FAITH!

Now faith is confidence in what we hope for and
assurance about what we do not see.
-Hebrews 11:1

LIKE MANY PEOPLE, I enjoy starting my day at the local coffee shop. The smell of fresh breakfast sandwiches fills the air while the steady hum of conversation surrounds me. People sip on their favorite "-chinos" and laugh with one another. The atmosphere is comfortable, even cozy. From my perspective, no one is worried. Everyone is enjoying one another's company, and life is great. But that's not everyone's reality.

If we could remove the curtain and see backstage into the lives of each person, we would see a more accurate picture. Each person has his or her own challenges, life issues, and difficulties. We would see how we *really* get through our daily lives, the decisions we make, and the why behind our choices. Ultimately, when everything is stripped away, it comes down to our faith.

The faith we have or don't have, our belief in the world and the way it works, and our thoughts about life beyond us are the forces that lead us every moment of every day. Some people don't realize this truth, some do. Regardless, it is our faith in something that guides us, whether that something is God, other people, our careers, our bank accounts, or anything else we trust to get us through life.

As I climb into bed at night, my mind makes a list of all the things I need to do the next day: a conference call with a friend, reply by email to one of our mission team members, remind my daughter about an appointment, send some work to another ministry partner ... the list goes on. Even the mental exercise of building that list requires faith. Faith that I will wake up in the morning. Faith that my computer will work. Faith that something won't happen that will prevent me from doing all of the above.

We act in faith every day. Some people may not call it faith, but in reality, that's what all of us exercise in our daily living. Without faith, why would we want to get out of the bed in the morning? What would be the purpose? We exercise faith because the Creator of the universe built within every human DNA this operational component that causes us to function by using faith. In fact, we can't function without it. It's how we run, much like how my car runs on gas. It can't operate without it. It can sit in the driveway. I can wash it and make it shine. The interior can be nice, and I can even sit in the car and listen to the radio, but it will *not* run without gas. Our lives are like that. We need that fuel of faith to operate. It's how God intended it to be.

STEP OUTSIDE or look out your window, and you will see faith in operation all around you. I see birds landing in the yard, pecking at the ground looking for food. Why did they land? They had faith food would be waiting. I see someone running down my street with ear buds in their ears. Why are they running? They are trying to stay in shape, and they have faith that running will help make that happen. It's different levels of faith, but faith nonetheless.

WHAT IS FAITH?

THE WRITER of Hebrews (11:1) defines faith as "confidence in what we hope for and assurance about what we do not see." That definition fits both what the bird and what the runner on my street demonstrated. The bird is confident there was food in the ground, even though he could not see; the runner is confident that running will help him stay in shape, even though he's not to his goal yet.

Even with these two examples right in front of me, I don't see much real confidence anymore. We have lost confidence in our country, our government, our church leaders, and one another. And probably for good reason. But that lack of confidence is a weapon of the enemy to cause us to give up—to give up based on what we see. The second part of the writer's definition is "assurance about what we do not see." It is easy to live by what we see, but that is not faith. Faith is believing even when we can't see. That's what Jesus told (Doubting) Thomas when he returned from the dead. Jesus said to him, *"Because you have seen me, you have believed, blessed are those who have not seen and yet have believed"* (John 20:29).

So, how can we gain that confidence and live with real faith? It starts with putting our faith in the right place. Because oftentimes it isn't that we don't have faith (although, sometimes we can lose our faith), but that our faith is placed in the incorrect thing—or maybe even the incorrect person.

Let me give you an example. Guys tend to put our misguided faith in two things. One is our job. As a friend of mine climbed the corporate ladder, he felt better about himself. His career became his obsession. When his job went belly-up, he suddenly realized his faith had been misplaced.

The other place we men sometimes put our faith is in our spouse or significant other. This is a hard one, because we're supposed to pledge ourselves unconditionally to our wife, and there is a certain amount of dependence that God's Word suggests as we become one and grow together. We cross the line when we put heavenly expectations on our earthly spouse. My wife, as awesome as she is, makes for a lousy God. She can't be *the* person in whom I put my entire faith and trust.

There is only one person qualified for that job. There is only one person who can handle that assignment. His name is Jesus.

In America, we tend to add something to our faith in Jesus. Jesus plus our job. Jesus plus our spouse. Jesus plus our kids. Jesus plus whatever. That, too, is misguided faith. Until we have faith in Jesus alone, we won't see the difference He wants to make in our lives.

CRAZY FAITH

WHEN WE PUT our full faith and trust in God, amazing things happen. I'm talking about the Hebrews 11:1, real, genuine, authentic kind of faith. We can come up with our own definition, but the Bible has defined it for us well. The New Living Translation says that "faith is the confidence that what we hope for will actually happen." It's not wishful thinking. It's total confidence in God. It's the kind of trust that Peter used to describe how he could be confident despite suffering. He said in 2 Timothy 1:12, "I know whom I have believed, and am persuaded that He is able to keep that which I've committed unto Him against that day." That persuasion—that belief—is an unconditional surrender of the heart and full reliance on God. Do we have it?

When we read verses like 2 Timothy 1:12 and give them serious thought, the attitude displayed by many of the people in Scripture seems somewhat ludicrous today, maybe even crazy. And yet, when we look at what God did in their lives, it took that kind of extraordinary faith in an extraordinary God to see extraordinary things happen. Maybe that is why we see few things that we would define as "extraordinary" today. We've become so accustomed to the mundane and ordinary. We've settled for half-hearted faith. Yet it's that Crazy Faith that makes all the difference.

Part of the challenge of living in America is the blessing of living in America. When we are blessed, we have need of nothing. When we have need of nothing, we aren't required to use as much faith. Because we can be our own provider, we've "got this." Part of the reason friends of mine have given up on the church and walked away is because they've never seen a life of Crazy Faith modeled for them. Why not? They've seen *American* faith instead. It's not until we can't fix something or get something done that we exercise Crazy Faith. Perhaps a crisis takes us to that point. Something has to be beyond our control in order for us to find that we remain totally dependent on God.

Back in the early 1990s, I experienced something like this that blew me away. I was in full-time ministry. My dear friend Jack Cleland and I were struggling. Both of us were recent newlyweds and both of us had one-car families. While juggling ministry trips and home life, we needed additional transportation, which neither of us could afford. We didn't know anyone else who could help us. Although we had been praying about it together and with our wives, we hadn't really shared our need with anyone else.

One day, a friend named Charlie gave us a call and said, "I'd like for the two of you to drive over to my home today if you have a minute." We knew Charlie fairly well, but we didn't talk that often. In fact, we hadn't talked in some time. When we arrived at his home, his wife greeted us at the door. "Come on in!"

We entered and followed her into the living room, where she motioned for us to take a seat. We did.

Charlie joined us with a smile and a hug. "Tell me about what God is doing with you guys and your ministry."

We shared for a while, and he asked if we had any needs right now. We talked a bit, and I really don't know if we even said anything about needing a car.

He stood up. "Come outside with me."

We walked outside, and he pulled some keys out of his pocket. "Guys, God has blessed us, and we seem to have two more cars than we do drivers here at our house. My wife and I have been praying, and God told us to give each of you one of these cars." He pointed at a

1980-something Honda Prelude and a 1980-something Honda CRX. "Now, obviously they aren't new. But they run well. They're Hondas, so they have room for another hundred-thousand miles or so. They've been serviced, and I'd like for you to have them. You guys can pick who

gets which one."

My friend and I stood there, speechless. Wow! We had been praying. We had exercised Crazy Faith that God would meet our need. And we trusted God had our backs and that He would provide. We hadn't told anyone that we could really use another car, and here was one person taking care of both our needs. I remember pulling out of his long, gravel driveway with tears streaming down my face and thanking God for looking out for me.

Sometimes I forget what it means to live by Crazy Faith. Looking back, I treasure those times. I want more of them in my life. Honestly, I want every day to be a day of Crazy Faith. I know that when I live with total surrender to God, I see him do things that blow my socks off!

If you are ready to live with that kind of faith, I want to encourage you by sharing some stories of other people who were tired of mundane, half-hearted faith and took the leap of Crazy Faith.

2

MIRACLES HAPPEN
Zechariah and Elizabeth
Jesus looked at them and said, "With man this is impossible, but not with
God; all things are possible with God."
-Mark 10:27

IN TODAY'S technologically advanced world, there are few people left who believe in miracles. Many people find excuses to write them off, and even those who claim to be Christ-followers sometimes react in surprise when they see God answer prayers that are way over the top. And yet, if we believe the words of Scripture, we know that God is a miracle-working God. Perhaps that belief itself requires us to step out in Crazy Faith. I'm coming off of one of those over-the-top prayers and God's answers this week.

A dear friend who interprets for us in the Dominican and serves as a missionary suddenly came down very ill and entered the hospital. This eighteen-year-old man was a picture of perfect health. He developed a high fever, his blood seemed to be pooling in certain areas of his arms, and the doctors were very concerned. When our family and friends here in the States found out, we sent out a plea for prayer to everyone we knew. More reports from the hospital began to come in. Words like "leukemia" were used. Soon they talked about spinal taps and chemotherapy. Our friends on the ground in Puerta Plata asked for more and more prayer. Christian radio stations began to share this with their listeners, asking them to join in prayer for healing. It seemed like the worst was yet to be.

But then. Don't you love those words?

Even better, *but God.*

The spinal tap results came back from the United States two days after Augusto, our Dominican missionary, had left the hospital feeling better and returned home. The results said his blood count was normal. No signs of anything. Doctors were left scratching their heads while his family and friends in the DR wept with joy. As news reached back to friends in the United States, people began to praise God. A miracle happened.

Personally, I believe that miracles happen every day. Sometimes we're too busy to see them. We run our hurried lives, striving to meet our own needs and, frankly, leave no room for God to work miracles that we would consider "legitimate." I think where God really wants us to live as Christ followers is to be so far out on the limb of Crazy Faith that God has to work miracles that we can see. Not in a careless way as if to try to make God work a miracle because we have stepped out in stupidity, but rather to live with such total surrender that we are dependent on the miraculous.

We find the story of this type of person in the gospel of Luke. Elizabeth is married to Zechariah and is hoping for a child. Zechariah is a member of the Jerusalem priesthood and Elizabeth, well ... she's well beyond child-bearing years. In fact, she was just past menopause, and her husband had given up on having a child. In those days, not having a child was looked upon as a disgrace. Zechariah felt hopeless. And Elizabeth ... she continued to pray and seek God.

It came about that Zechariah was at the temple to offer a sacrifice, chosen by random lot to enter the sanctuary. Or so it seemed. It was nothing but divinely orchestrated by God. Nothing is random with God.

When God asks you to step out in Crazy Faith, rest assured, He has been and is working behind the scenes.

ZECHARIAH WAS the single priest that could enter the sanctuary. God had chosen him and set him apart from 8,000 other priests. God had a specific assignment and a specific task ordained for Zechariah.

When I was in high school, I wanted a part-time job so I could make a little extra money. I applied at a new burger chain that was opening in town. I was hoping to get a job cleaning, working in the ice cream area—anything but cooking.

After the interview, the owner said, "Congratulations, you've got the job! I'm going to put you on the grill."

The grill. Ugh! That's the last thing I wanted.

A week later, on our invitation-only opening night, that's where I was—flipping burgers. The heat was intense. There were four of us on the grill, and the serving line was right behind us so that people could watch as we cooked the food. Curtis, the guy beside me on the grill, was nervous; he needed the job to pay for college.

To shake off the nervousness and help him focus on cooking, I made a suggestion. "Let's sing some while we cook."

"Sing?" he shot back. "Have you lost your mind?"

One of the other guys looked over at me and said, "Sounds fun. What we singin'?"

A few minutes later, the cook crew was singing "My Girl" by the Temptations, much to the delight and applause of those in line. Later that evening, as we were closing up, the owner came over to me. I knew I was in trouble. Instead, he said, "You guys sounded great and the people loved it." He slapped me on the back and walked off.

My friend, Curtis, came running over. "What did he say?"

"He said the people loved it!" I said while grinning.

Curtis grinned back and began to laugh. "Thanks for getting me through opening night, man."

"You bet." I walked away that night thanking God for putting me on the grill, letting me sing like a fool, and making a new friend. God had put me right where he wanted me. Just like he did for Zechariah.

When Zechariah entered the temple, an angel appeared to give him some astonishing news. The angel told Zechariah that his wife would have a son.

Haven't we heard this story before?

But Zechariah doubted the word of the angel. He almost objected and asked for a sign (just like Abraham did in Genesis 15:8). Because Zechariah doubted the word from the Lord, he was punished. God turned him deaf and mute. Upon leaving the temple, he couldn't talk. The people realized something remarkable had happened, but they were unsure what.

Soon, Elizabeth received a visit from Mary, Jesus's mother. At that moment, Elizabeth's baby kicked in her womb. And not too much later, Elizabeth gave birth to her baby boy, a miracle before her very eyes.

On the eighth day of circumcision, tradition held that the baby was given a name. Boys were customarily named after their grandfather. Zechariah and Elizabeth's family gathered together. Elizabeth's family suggested the baby be named Zechariah, after his dad, but Elizabeth objected. God had already given her the child's name. She said, "He is to be named John."

The family argued and looked to Zechariah to settle the argument, but he still couldn't speak. Someone handed him a writing tablet, and he sketched out the words, "His name is John." At that moment, his ability to speak returned and he praised God. At the sound of his voice, the neighbors were silenced. They were perplexed and puzzled.

The praises of one following God in Crazy Faith will often silence the crowd around us.

ELIZABETH AND ZECHARIAH were excited about the birth of their son. Elizabeth especially knew that God had big plans for her son. Her baby would grow up to be John the Baptist, the one to announce the coming of the Messiah. Looking at the story on this side of history, it's easy to miss out on some of the questions Elizabeth and Zechariah might have been asking themselves in the midst of all this. They had their doubts, and yet God was patient. And God did immeasurably more than they could have thought. Which just goes to show, God's plans are always better than ours. He knows exactly where we need to be.

PERSONAL APPLICATION

- Are you looking for a miracle? Do you have Crazy Faith?
- Are you willing for God to set you apart so that you can live with crazy faith?
- Are you willing to let God supply the support you need like he supplied Mary to be the support for Elizabeth?
- Are you willing to let God be the one that silences the naysayers and you focus on doing what God has called you to do?

Make a promise to God to be set apart for Him.

But you are not like that, for you are a chosen people. You are royal priests,
a holy nation, God's very own possession.

1 Peter 2:9

3

I KNOW WHOM I BELIEVE
Mike and Terica Williams
"...because I know whom I have believed, and I am convinced that he is able
to guard what I have entrusted to him until that day."
-2 Timothy 1:12

WHEN I THINK of Zechariah and Elizabeth, I think of my friends Mike and Terica Williams. Mike and Terica are being used by God to make an impact in the lives of kids in the Dominican Republic. Their work, like the work of Zechariah and Elizabeth, is paving the way for kids to encounter the hope of Jesus.

Mike traveled the country for years doing comedy, making people laugh even while he was pointing them to God. Everyone loved Mike and his humor, and he was making a good living doing it. Then, one day, God asked him to ignore the applause and step out in Crazy Faith. This is his story.

∾

FOG HOVERS eerily low over the surface of the dark, mysterious river. The natives call it the River of Blood because of the lives that have been taken into its depths and never allowed to return. It could be the crocodiles, or it could be the piranhas. It could be the anacondas that call this ebb and flow their home. The missionaries see this river as the gospel hi-way. Unfortunately, the gospel has yet to reach it all. There is much danger here. The grandsons of the headhunters, uncivilized, continue to commit brazen attacks.

I sit on the bank, worried about a small cut on my ankle. Will the piranhas really go into a frenzy if I have to step into the river? I keep reminding myself that I am divinely protected, for I am on a mission for God. But then again, I read the Jim Elliot story, and I watched the movie, *The Edge of the Spear*. Neither ended well, and I think Jim Elliot was a more spiritually devout man than I.

I kind of wish the words above were my story. It may be what you want to hear when you are reading about a missionary. I feel like a sluggard. My first mission adventure involved an American Airlines jet, and I paid the additional ninety dollars for an upgrade to first class.

My God-call came when a friend of mine was going to visit a mission his father and mother had started in Haiti. He would only be there for a few days.

"Hey Mike, do you wanna ride shotgun on a sugar cane wagon?" he asked.

It sounded like fun. I love to ride shotgun. I had never been on a sugar cane wagon. I had never been to the third world before, unless you consider West Virginia the third world. I replied, "Let's go!"

In Haiti, we visited the poorest villages I have ever seen. We played music for the locals on our guitars and they played for us. We prayed for the sick. We fed the hungry. We touched the hurting. Driving out at the end of that week, I cried as I waved goodbye to the miles of hungry eyes waving back at me. Hopelessness had a home; it was on the Island of Hispaniola, ninety air-minutes off the southern tip of Florida. As we drove, I thought to myself that I would prefer not to return to this place again. I would give money to help, but I never wanted to see it, smell it, touch it, or taste it again. This is too close. Nevertheless, God had other plans.

I was never able to get that trip out of my mind. Trust me, I tried. Why would God want me there? I would not make a good missionary. I'm a comedian. My spiritual gift is sarcasm. I am well versed to stand up in front of crowds and make them laugh for ninety minutes and go home. I don't think I can help people laugh their hunger away. If laughter could quench hunger, I would not be fat. And—another reason I asked why God would want me there—I was making a real nice living telling these jokes.

For a while, I quenched the call by raising a lot of money for that mission. I convinced myself that was best of both worlds. However, the yearning inside kept pulling me to a boots-on-the-ground position. Elizabeth Elliot said, "Patience in God is this: Not having any agenda of my own, no deadlines, no demands on what God must do. But simply having open hands and open hearts, ready to receive what God would choose, and a perfect confidence that what He chooses will be better than my best." I have come to learn that God does not need my money, nor does he need my boots on the ground. But I need to be doing what He wants me to do when He wants me to do it.

It was but a few months later that my wife and I put our house on the market, had a big garage sale, packed our bags, and moved to the Island of Hispaniola. Hispaniola is the island that contains two countries. One third is Haiti, the poorest country in the eastern hemisphere, and two-thirds is the Dominican Republic, the most human-trafficked country in the eastern hemisphere. Both are considered among the most corrupt governments in the free world. So it seemed like a great idea to raise our four children there. Um ... not at all. But when God calls you to go anywhere—across the world or across the street—you have a choice. What will you do? Let's be honest. Safety anywhere is really just a dream. If you don't believe me, please watch the news tonight.

Looking years back now, I still remember the day we landed at that little airport with twelve suitcases, six backpacks, and a guitar. We had no financial support. We were following a New Testament style of mission funding made popular by the apostle Paul called tent-making. Paul, to support his mission work, would make tents and sell them. I have no idea how big they were. Maybe they were pup tents, family tents, or circus tents, for that matter. I don't know. I do know that he was willing to put in his own sweat equity to do what God had called him to do. We had chosen to do the same. Using the time many missionaries would come home on furlough, I would choose to come home and tell jokes to raise our needed support. God willing?

We had little idea of what God wanted us to accomplish. Had we known the large scale of His plan, I would have most likely chickened out. My visions are usually much smaller than His designs. I build birdhouses. God creates trees and then forests. Today we find ourselves operating a mission that serves hundreds of people. We serve a very poor, rural mountain-top area where the children are the targets of sex traffickers. We are trying to rescue a whole lot of girls from certain destruction.

Among the poor there is a tragic fairy tale. The story tells of the young teenage girl who goes to town and meets a foreign man. She pleases him in every way he asks. He comes to visit her again and again. One day this foreign man takes her back to America or Germany or Spain, and the girl lives happily ever after in a big, fancy house. Now because she is rich, she can send money back to her very poor family and her brothers and sisters can have a better life. How tragic is this lie? How many young girls follow the tragic fairy tale and end up the discards of the perverts that visit our shores? Our mission programs empower young girls to make choices for success that don't include selling themselves.

We also have the joy of bringing relief to the Haitian refugees living in the dump. These poorest of the poor lost their homes during an earthquake. Now they live in squalor. What can a Jesus follower do? Through the small gifts of people in the United States, we are able to continue an ongoing feeding ministry program bringing hot soup, peanut butter sandwiches, and cold, clean water to those people. It has been our joy to serve these dear humble people, as many of them call Jesus Christ their Savior and Lord.

God has allowed us to build houses and build bridges. We have been able to touch the lives of deaf children and bring glasses to those whose eyes were becoming blind in old age. We have helped start businesses for widows and install roofs for families. We have been able to join God on some of the greatest adventures you could imagine.

Sure there have been hurts along the way. Some days we weep. I can tell you of the thirteen-year-old girl whose mother has been selling her to a neighbor since she was eight years old. How did this slip past us? Now she is pregnant, and the school doesn't allow pregnant girls to attend. What do I say to her? We hold her hand and promise to be there from now on.

I think of Wendis, who is sixteen. An old padlock secures her three-year-old child behind that wooden door of their single-room shack as Wendis heads out to find someone who will buy her for enough food to feed her and her child. You can look the other way when you don't know their name, but when you know their name, it's not so easy. She brings her little boy to our Bible programs. Wendis sits with the children and tries to live the childhood she never received.

There are days that the work seems so big and brings us to tears, but we get up the next morning ready to charge the gates of hell again. Why? Because we have chosen to join God in making a difference, not just making a statement.

The Crossover Cups Mission is not an isolated case. There are people all around the world who have been so crazy in their faith in Jesus to follow Him wherever He would lead. I want to encourage you to follow the calling God has placed on your life. I want to read your God-story in a book someday.

The words of the old missionary C.T. Studd speak to me today.

"Some wish to live within the should-of church or chapel bell, I want to run a rescue ship within a yard of hell."

COME SEE first-hand what the team is doing in the Dominican. The Crossover Cups Mission lives serving the poorest of the poor day in and day out. Young girls are being rescued every day; many are coming to know Jesus. It's that kind of Crazy Faith.

4

WHAT A PROCLAMATION!
Elijah
I exalt You, my God the King,
and praise Your name forever and ever.
² I will praise You every day;
I will honor Your name forever and ever.
-Psalm 145:1-2

ONE OF MY favorite stories recorded in the Scriptures is the story of Elijah and the false prophets of Baal. It's found in 1 Kings 18. In Elijah's time, culture defined what God was, and one lone soldier in God's army stood tall with his decree that God was the One True God. We need that kind of boldness in the world. We need that kind of Crazy Faith.

Israel had not received any rain for more than three years. The people found themselves in this predicament because they had committed idolatry ... again. This seemed to be a constant theme for the people of Israel: follow God, praise God, turn to idols, face punishment, repent, follow God, praise God... And God judged them according to their sin. I have to admit: this looks familiar in my own life at times.

God speaks to Elijah and tells him to confront King Ahab. As a result, He will send the rain that is desperately needed.

Elijah confronts King Ahab and challenges him to a duel. Elijah tells the king to gather all of Israel at Mt. Carmel, along with all the false prophets of Baal, 450 of them. And if that's not enough, Elijah asked for the 400 prophets of the false goddess Asherah to join them. Once they were assembled together, Elijah charged the people with a question: "How long will you waver between two opinions? If the Lord is God, follow Him; but if Baal is God, follow him."

Stepping out in Crazy Faith will often have you standing against the opposition.

WHAT WE HAVE HERE IS the state of lukewarm-ness. John mentions something similar in the book of Revelation. The people of Israel were being two-faced, using God when it was convenient to do so while serving themselves when they wanted to. Elijah steps out in Crazy Faith to challenge the status quo. As oftentimes happens when someone is brave enough to do this, the people remained quiet and noncommittal.

When you follow God in Crazy Faith, be prepared for times of silence.

ELIJAH THEN CHALLENGED the false prophets of Baal to prepare an offering for their god, while he would do the same. The stipulation: they could light no fire on the altar. Elijah told the people, "The God who answers with fire from heaven ... He is the One True God." All of Israel was gathered—almost 1,000 false prophets, a noncommittal crowd, and one person who has chosen to believe in the One True God. What an act of Crazy Faith!

When I was in tenth grade, there was a very similar situation in my English class. No, there weren't hundreds of false prophets involved. In fact, there was only one: a high school English teacher. The class had been reading a literature story. I don't remember which one it was, but it could have been something about mythology. It had a part about the reincarnation of some god. A young girl in the class had an inquisitive look on her face after the teacher read that paragraph.

"What's the problem, Kathy?" the teacher asked.

"I'm not sure I agree with this story," Kathy shyly responded.

"What do you mean you don't agree?"

"That's not true stuff," Kathy replied. "I don't believe that."

"Why not?"

"Because I am a Christian."

What? Did she really say that out loud? Granted, it was 1986, but still. I could feel the sudden shudder in the room. She'd just brought religion into English class. *Uh oh. Here it comes.*

"You're a Christian?" the teacher asked, as she laughed and shook her head in disbelief. "So you believe the Bible, then?" The teacher continued to poke fun.

"Yes, I do," Kathy said. I could tell she was trying to put some strength behind her words.

"Well, well, does anyone else here agree with Kathy?"

You could have heard a pin drop. Many people looked down at their desks for fear of being called on. Many others laughed and smiled with the teacher. But when she asked the question, there was silence. No response. No answer. No noise, until—

"I have to say that I agree with her," I responded quietly. I knew I had just earned myself a failing grade and would be taking this class next semester. Another year of English? Yuck.

"Oh you do, Mr. Eason," she said. She laughed even louder.

My heart pounded. I heard the students' laughter mingle with the teacher's. Tears formed in Kathy's eyes and she ducked her head, her chin rested against her chest. I knew I had a decision to make. I was just about to respond further when the teacher shouted out again.

"And I guess that story of Jonah being swallowed by the big huge fish that's in there ... you believe that too, huh?"

I could feel the conviction welling up within me. She turned her back and walked to the blackboard.

"As a matter of fact, I do. And if it said that Jonah was the one that swallowed the big fish, I would believe that too!" I said, proud of the strength in my voice, grateful that my nervousness hadn't cracked it.

Kathy's head lifted. Her tears stopped and her eyes met mine. A tentative smile spread across her face. At that moment, the other students who'd lowered their heads and averted their eyes sat straighter. Those who were laughing quieted.

The teacher turned around in slow motion. "Humph." She went to her desk and sat down.

At that moment, thankfully, the bell rang, and everyone hurriedly excited the class.

As I stood to leave, Kathy grabbed my arm and said "thank you" before she slipped out of the classroom. I learned that day that it takes a lot of courage and a lot of

Crazy Faith to stand against the crowd, whether the crowd is one or a thousand.

Stepping out in Crazy Faith often will often have you standing all by yourself.

THE PEOPLE AGREED to the rules of the contest, and Elijah allowed the false prophets to go first. The pagans cried out and danced around the altar from early in the morning until high noon. Nothing happened. Crickets. All quiet. Their god didn't respond.

Elijah decided to mock them and have a little fun. "Shout louder!" he screamed at them. "Surely he is a god!"

Notice he didn't say, "Surely he *is God.*"

He taunted the false prophets even more when their god still failed to answer. "Maybe he is in deep thought, busy, or traveling; maybe he is asleep..." Elijah barked.

Still *no answer.*

At one point, Elijah said, "Maybe your god is in the bathroom!"

Check out the translation. He is so *sure* his God is the One True God.

Confidence in the One True God results in Crazy Faith.

THE PROPHETS of Baal shouted louder and cut themselves, trying to get the attention of their god. Midday came and went and evening approached, and still *nothing.* No one listened. No one paid attention. No one answered. The false prophets began to sweat.

Then Elijah called all the people around and repaired the altar. He used twelve stones to build a trench around the altar. After he placed wood on it, brought an animal to the altar, and cut the pieces of the bull to be placed on it, he asked the people to douse the altar with water. The people took twelve large jars of water and doused the altar.

"Do it again," Elijah commanded them.

The people doused it a second time.

Do it again," Elijah shouted again.

The people doused it a third time. There was so much water that the sacrifice was soaked and water ran over the trench. The altar practically sat in a swimming pool.

Can you imagine what was going through the minds of the people? Either this guy had completely lost it, or ...? All eyes were on Elijah. Elijah's eyes were on his God.

Elijah, after the sacrifice was ready, prayed to God. "Lord, the God of Abraham, Isaac, and Israel, let it be known today that you are God in Israel and that I am your servant and have done all these things at Your command. Answer me, Lord, answer me, so that these people will know that You, Lord, are God, and that You are turning their hearts back again."

The fire of the Lord fell from heaven and consumed the burnt offering. And the fire consumed the wood. And the fire consumed the stones. The stones ... the rocks ... consumed them. *And* consumed the dust ... *and* licked up all the water in the trench. False Prophets - 0. God - 1. In that moment, the people of Israel bowed in reverence and declared the Lord as the One True God.

Stepping out in Crazy Faith will always have you amazed at God.

ELIJAH THEN TOLD the people to put the false prophets to death, and the Lord sent rain upon the land. Elijah's prayers had been answered. God had heard. God listened. God responded.

Confidence that results in Crazy Faith comes from communion with God.

ELIJAH HAD BEEN PRAYING. In order for us to develop Crazy Faith, we have to commune consistently with God. We can't allow interruptions to keep us from our time with Him. That's where confidence for the journey comes from: fellowship and communion with God. Have you ever noticed that the more time we spend with someone, the more confidence we get in that relationship? The same is true with our relationship with God. The more time we spend with Him, the more we will trust His Word. Our belief will become greater in His Word, and we will gain the confidence that causes us to live in Crazy Faith.

PERSONAL APPLICATION

How confident are you in God? Here are a few questions to consider:

- Where is God asking me to demonstrate Crazy Faith?
- Have I talked with God about this area? Consistently?
- How is my daily communion with God?
- Am I ready to demonstrate confidence in an awesome God?

Your trust in God will be the fuel to follow Him with Crazy Faith.

So then faith comes by hearing, and hearing by the word of God.
Romans 10:17

5

FORGIVENESS: *Shelley Armato*
If we confess our sins, he is faithful and just and will forgive us our sins and purify us from all unrighteousness.
I John 1:9

I love hearing a story about someone who could have taken the path heavily traveled and who could have lived in past regret. But then this person makes the decision to take what happened in the past and use it as a stepping stone, a platform to champion the cause of Christ, even though doing so may be painful and cause unwanted attention.

Shelley Armato was almost seventeen years old. Her life had been defined by a series of events that left her feeling worthless and hopeless. She was searching for love with the only thing she had to offer—giving her body away. She believed that no one would ever want anything of her other than using her for physical gratification. While all this inner turmoil was going on, the Roe vs. Wade bill had just been passed. Newscasts around the country were proclaiming the legalization of abortion. The headlines touted, "Finally Women's Rights!" This is her story.

It was perfect timing for me. I felt I had nowhere to turn. I could not confide in my mother; she had taken enough beatings in her life, and this would be just one more reason for my father to attack her. So that door was closed.

I had heard all my life that I was worthless and would never be anything. My grandparents even wrote me out of their will. Money was for men, and women in my family were less than the dirt under their feet. My perception of myself was flawed from the beginning. I had a burning desire for connection and love. And there were a lot of men who would oblige me. Only now I found myself pregnant, in fear, and alone.

After this horrific event, I never spoke of it. I would not dream of ever allowing anyone to know what happened. It was a quick, thirty-minute procedure that defined the next thirty years of my life. I harbored shame, guilt, and a legacy of unforgiveness. My heart was heavy. I had adopted a mask that held people at bay even while it kept me lonely and fearful that someone would find out.

A mere $200 came with a lifetime of regret. Shame and guilt are the worst emotions, but I live with them long enough they became my friend. Drugs and alcohol could only squash the feelings for a brief time. For a few blessed minutes I could be free from the pain and everything was alright, but the second I sobered up, it was there again. But it was only a temporary numbing of the pain that would come right back. Staring me in the face. Waiting for me to respond.

My journey is one of finding understanding, forgiveness, and love. In 2009, I was nominated as a Fearless Business Woman. I had moved on from my past mistakes and was now making a difference in the community as a business leader. At the event to celebrate my nomination, I was asked to come up on stage. The crowd was watching as I was handed the microphone and asked what legacy I would like to leave my children. For most of the other women, it was money. For me, I stood proudly and said, "Jesus Christ, because with Him, all things are possible." The crowd gasped as one entity. This was a business event; no one was bold enough to proclaim His word over money. I was now publicly outed as a follower of Jesus. I took my seat, proud of holding to my convictions, and the evening continued.

Shortly after that evening, a lady connected with me and asked me to attend an event in California. This lady was hosting it and teaching other ladies how to become an authentic speaker. It was six days of peeling the onion and learning to speak from your heart. I went, not knowing what to expect, but eager to learn. On the last day, we had two minutes to share a story. It was on that stage my absence of the truth came out.

I stood and told a politically correct story and received a standing ovation. I stepped off the stage and cried uncontrollably for thirty minutes. I knew I had missed an opportunity. I also knew I had let God down, but even more I had let myself down. Deep within, I knew the truth had to be set free. I was standing next to a lady, so I looked at her and said, "I am going to start a movement of women who stand in their God-given power and live free from judgment and change this world with forgiveness."

Out of that experience, The Courage Coalition was born. After much prayer, I decided to hold a two-day event on June 30 - July 1 and invite women from around the world to come to our city to share their authentic stories, not knowing at the time all the planning was really for my own story. I was merely acting on faith that God would provide me with what I was to share and what the event was to look like.

As I planned the event, God began bringing women to me. They had a need for a venue, a sacred place to be heard. They wanted a voice that could change the world. I believed that authenticity was key. We would only change the world if people knew we were real. The planning was amazing.

We had 115 women come to share their story. As I sat in the back of the room watching and listening, I was in awe of the power of testimony; every one of the stories told of Jesus protecting them and providing for them. That was the first day I found my courage.

I stopped the planned program and asked my friend, Stephanie

Tillman, to join me on the stage. She was unaware of my past. She didn't have a clue what I was about to share. My heart was pounding out of my chest. But I knew I had to speak out as each of the other women had done. I told my true story in front of 100 women. Little did I know the impact I would have on the audience that had gathered that day. The event stopped. God had brought several women to the venue to be healed, and tears began to flow. We leaned on each other, formed circles of love and joy, and danced in our sorrow.

Now for the big problem. I had just told all these women this huge thing, and no one else really knew. Especially not my children. So I knew I had to ask for their forgiveness.

The first one I chose to tell was my oldest son; he was in the Navy. I called him and asked him to come home for the weekend, and he jumped on a plane and flew home. He was standing at the counter in my kitchen, six-foot-five inches tall, a gorgeous man with a huge heart. I swallowed hard and told him of my terrible decision when I was so young. He walked around the counter and hugged me like I have never been hugged.

He looked me in the eye and said, "Mom, I love you. I am so proud of you!"

Through tears, I responded, "The crazy thing is God still trusted me with you!"

I had been blessed beyond my wildest dreams, and I asked him to forgive me, for my shame had defined my parenting.

Next, I had to tell my youngest son, William. I call him Dr. Will for Dr. Phil; he has great wisdom and knowledge. I think I should have named him Solomon. He is also a six-foot-five young man and is a drummer in the church band.

Soon after telling my oldest son, my youngest and I were driving one afternoon. My mind raced. How would I tell him? I burst into tears.

He stopped the car as he asked me what was wrong, and I told him everything was finally right. I looked over at him and shared the same story with him.

Will got out of the car and asked, "Mom, do you need to go see my pastor?"

"I'm good with God. I just needed to ask you for your forgiveness," I replied. "I'm glad God still trusted me with you."

He hugged me again and looked me in the eye. "Go tell the world. Don't let this ever happen to anyone again!"

Wow, what a relief!

Now I had to tell my daughter. She has two children of her own. Tatum is a wisdom-filled woman, beautiful and driven.

Time was not on my side; she knew many of the women at the event. I didn't want her to hear this through the grapevine, so I knew I had to be aggressive. I asked her out to lunch.

On the drive to lunch and through my tears, I told her the same story I had told her brothers. Again, I told her how amazed I was that God still trusted me with her. We sat in silence for some time as I wondered what she was going to say.

Then she looked at me. "Do you want to go have lunch?"

That was it! Each of my children forgave me and extended grace and mercy. I was so thankful. When I think of what it took for me to be honest about my past, Crazy Faith comes to mind.

Then, a letter had to be written to the unborn baby.

Dear little child of mine,

I hold you in my heart. I am in awe of your spirit that still lives in me; your love is so bold, your beauty so great. Each and every day I praise God for you and the wisdom you bring me. Please forgive me for the terrible choice I made. You are a child of mine. My heart aches with pain, yet my soul rejoices knowing of your presence.

For some this will be read in disdain. Women in your life are hurting, and judgment will come back to you. Others will be set free from their own pain. Some will not realize the impact on their life from a decision. God still loves us; He holds us in the palm of his hand. He delights in giving to us. He died on the cross for our sins, so many and so great.

Loving others out loud is my life's work, and holding a space for others to stand in their authenticity is my joy. I'm so grateful God gave me the Crazy Faith to share my story with others.

SHELLEY CONTINUES to share her story, and her business continues to make great strides in enabling her to speak life into people in all walks of life. Her Crazy Faith is making an impact every day.

6

COURAGEOUS LEADERSHIP: *Moses*
Be strong and of good courage, do not fear nor be afraid of them; for the
LORD your God, He is the One who goes with you.
-Deuteronomy 31:6

MOSES WAS PERHAPS one of the greatest heroes in the Bible. His is one of those stories that tells of the underdog who comes back to be a mighty weapon in the hand of God. His story is full of Crazy Faith.

Long before Moses was born, the children of Israel were living in slavery. Egypt was their homeland. But as the numbers of the Israelites grew, Pharaoh feared they would soon grow into an army that would come to overtake his kingdom. As a result, he put them under extreme bondage and issued a decree that all the male children were to be killed. It was at this time that Moses was born.

Moses' mother hid him for the first three months of his life out of fear of him being found and killed by Pharaoh or his army. As her fear increased and Moses' whereabouts became more likely, she put her three-month-old son in a miniature ark—a basket made of bulrushes—and placed him down by the river bank, praying and believing that he might be found and thus, spared.

Little did she know, in God's divine providence, it would be the Pharaoh's daughter who would find Moses when she went down to the river to bathe. When Pharaoh's daughter found the baby, she realized he would need someone to nurse him. So she sought out someone to do so. The Pharaoh's daughter found Moses' mother and asked her to nurse the child.

God returned Moses to his mother. Amazing.

Often times, when you give up something for God, it results in your blessing.

WHEN THE NURSING stage was over, the Pharaoh's daughter took him, and he was raised up in Pharaoh's house as a son of the king.

As Moses matured, he became very upset seeing his fellow Hebrews treated badly. So upset, in fact, that when he saw an Egyptian beating a fellow Hebrew, he flew off the handle and killed the Egyptian. He fled after this experience. Pharaoh found out about the Egyptian's death, and Moses fled, fearing for his life. This flight took him out to the desert for forty years, where he ran headlong into God. Forty years...

Crazy Faith takes time to build.

AFTER HIS PEOPLE wandered through the desert for forty years, God heard their cries and decided to speak to Moses. God used a bush to get his attention. As it burned with fire, Moses was astonished. The fire never consumed it. "Moses, I have heard the cries of my people!" God spoke from the midst of the fiery bush.

Moses was even more amazed when God told him that he would be the one who would deliver His people out of Egypt. Moses freaked out. This was something Moses wasn't prepared to hear. He asked God the question anyone would have asked.

"Who am I ... that I could bring the people out of Egypt?"

God made a grand statement to Moses after promising His presence in the process. He told Moses to tell the people that the name of their God was "I AM who I AM." Then, God added four more important instructions for Moses to follow.

1. Tell the people "I am the God of their fathers—Abraham, Isaac, and Jacob—and I will deliver My people into the Promised Land flowing with milk and honey."
2. "Approach the Pharaoh and tell him to let My people go into the wilderness for a three-day journey into the Promised Land."
3. "Pharaoh will not let you go the first time you ask. If he doesn't let you go, tell him I will stretch out My hand and strike Egypt will all of My wonders."
4. "After I stretch out My hand with all these wonders, Pharaoh *will* let you go."

After Moses heard all the words from God, Moses *still* questioned Him. That gives me great encouragement, personally. I used to feel bad that after hearing instructions from the Lord, I would occasionally still question God as to the authenticity of them. And yet, even after God had laid out many promises, Moses still didn't hesitate to ask, "What if they don't believe me?"

With patience, the Lord God gave Moses further instructions. "Take the rod you are holding and throw it on the ground!"

Moses did, and the rod turned into a serpent.

God then said, "Pick up the serpent by the tail."

Moses reached down to pick up the serpent, and when he did, it turned back into the rod.

But God wasn't finished yet. "Place your hand into your bosom and take it out again."

Moses's hand became leprous.

"Place your hand back into your bosom again," God commanded.

Moses's hand was restored.

God also told Moses that if he still met disbelief, Moses was to take some water from the river and pour it onto the ground. The water would turn into blood.

After seeing all of this, Moses, incredibly, remained unsure. He made more excuses. "G-G-God, I'm not a g-g-g-reat speaker. I'm not sure I am the right man for the job."

"Who has made man's mouth?" the Lord asked. "Have not I, the Lord? Now therefore, go, and I will be with your mouth and teach you what you will say."

Moses had one final appeal for God. "O my Lord, please ... send by the hand of whomever else You may send."

Not a good response, given all the things the Lord said. After all this instruction and Moses's continual excuses, wasn't it possible that the Lord's patience may have worn thin? It did, but God was gracious and told Moses that he could take Aaron with him. Moses and his brother gathered the people and headed to meet the Pharaoh for a showdown, prepared with Crazy Faith.

Moses spent time with God. They communicated. Many people run out to do something—supposedly for God—and say they are exercising Crazy Faith, when actually, they are only exercising the crazy part. How do we know the difference? How do we determine, *discern* that what we think God is telling us is really God and not the bad pizza we ate the night before?

Moses gives us the answer: by spending time and communicating with God. I think that's why God was patient. Moses wanted to make absolutely certain he was hearing from God and not having a psychotic episode. He knew people, even his fellow Hebrews, would question his direction.

Needless to say, as God had warned Moses, the Pharaoh refused to respond to Moses's request. Moses, in an effort to change Pharaoh's mind, threw his rod down in front of Pharaoh and his entourage. The rod became a serpent. Unexpectedly, the magicians in Pharaoh's court threw down their rods, which also became serpents. Not to be outdone and to prove His mighty power, God caused Moses's serpent to turn on the other serpents and destroy them.

The king was angered at God's power, and his heart hardened. He would not allow the God of Moses to win the battle.

At this point, God had no choice but to release a full-scale assault on the Pharaoh that would cause him to eventually break and grant the request of Moses. Ten plagues were sent to change Pharaoh's mind. (Read the account in Exodus 12-14.) These plagues in and of themselves continued to demonstrate the awesome power of God and the Crazy Faith of this Hebrew underdog.

Pharaoh—physically, mentally, and emotionally defeated— finally relented and agreed to let Moses and the Hebrew people leave captivity. After 430 years, the Hebrew people were freed from Egyptian rule.

Just because something has been a certain way for a long period of time doesn't mean it has to stay that way.

CRAZY FAITH CAN BE DEFINED as being willing to change the status quo and think outside the box.

The Israelites, led by Moses, started on their journey to freedom. As the Israelites left, Pharaoh had another sudden change of heart. He decided to pursue them and kill as many as he could, including Moses.

The Israelites doubted Moses and wondered about the promises of God. After *everything*, why would God do this? Why would He let them be recaptured? And possibly killed? They were stuck at the edge of the Red Sea with nowhere to go. No escape. Out of resources. No more options. Frantic, their doubts and complaining began.

The Egyptian army was closing in. What could Moses do?

Have you ever been in a position similar to Moses'? Have you felt like your options were running out?

One year, our family felt like God was calling us to move. We weren't exactly sure where; we just knew we were going to be moving. We put our house up for sale and started to pack things we didn't need. Then the economy tanked. We had relocated part of our ministry to Nashville, Tennessee, while we lived in South Carolina. As God began to speak to our hearts, we just assumed we would be going to Nashville. But our house would not sell.

After almost a year of running up and down the interstate and with the economy worsening, I questioned the authenticity of God's instructions. "God, what are you doing? Did I hear you clearly?"

All the while, the radio division of our ministry continued to suffer and the writing on the wall became clearer as to its future. As we closed the doors on our radio division, I shook my head in disbelief, wondering about God's instructions. My wife and I still felt like God had told us to prepare to move. About that time, a pastor-friend in Knoxville called and asked me about helping their church through an interim time by leading music on Sundays.

My wife and I prayed about it. I agreed to help for a few weeks, and as I did, I quickly developed a love of their people. My wife enjoyed them too. As the weekly, three-hour trip from home started to become a chore, we looked at each other. Maybe we *were* moving to Tennessee. Maybe it was Knoxville, not Nashville.

The church leadership and personnel team asked me to consider taking over permanently. "God, is this where you are leading?" we prayed. The pastor and I were dear friends. My wife could work from anywhere. My kids were homeschooled at the time.

But our house would not sell. We changed realtors; we spent money fixing the things the new realtor said to fix. Weeks passed. Still no "SOLD" sign out front.

Finally, we told the pastor and church in Knoxville that we needed to say "no" to their invitation and allow the church to move forward with other possible candidates for the job. At this point, I felt like a failure. Had I heard from God? Where was He? Why did He allow my family all this grief and upheaval if we weren't moving?

My kids got stir crazy. The packed boxes in the garage slowly came back inside. And then—

Our realtor called. "Someone wants to look at your house today ... in about thirty minutes," she said.

My wife hung up the phone. She looked at me.

"Don't even clean up. They aren't interested. They aren't going to buy it. Let's go," I said with frustration. We jumped in the car and drove away.

We came back about an hour later, and the realtor called. "They want in by the end of the month!"

We. Were. Moving!

But we didn't land in Tennessee. We landed in South Carolina, about thirty-five miles from our old house. But, we did move! And we are already seeing God's hand on His timing.

So, what did Moses do?

Moses stepped up to lead. He valiantly grabbed his rod—filled with hope—and told the Israelites, *"Do not be afraid, stand still, and see the salvation of the Lord, which He will accomplish for you today. The Egyptians you see today, you will see no more. The Lord will fight for you, and you shall hold your peace"* (Exodus 14:13-14).

We read those verses on this side of history, sometimes out of context, and wonder, "How could Moses take such a stand?" That's why it's important to read the whole story in context. When you do, you read about Moses's many questions to God and God's answers. And despite Moses's continued push-back, God honored each word He told Moses. So, when Moses got to this point, he didn't know the *how*, but he knew that God would deliver the Israelites, for God *never* breaks His promises. Someone with Crazy Faith always remembers: *God* never *breaks His promises.* He may not answer our requests the way we think He should, but if God has promised something, He will deliver. Moses knew that.

Next, Moses lifted his rod as the Lord told him to do, stretched his hand over the sea, and the waters began to part. The Red Sea opened up and left dry ground to walk upon. Moses and the Israelites crossed over with a wall of water on their left and one on their right. I'm sure the people were astonished. I imagine there was laughter and tears. Thankfulness. Gratitude. Rejoicing.

But the Egyptian army headed toward them on the same passageway. What would God do? What would Moses do?

After the Israelites had safely crossed the Red Sea, God told Moses to lift the rod again. At that moment, the waters returned, covering the chariots and Pharaoh's army. In one incredible act of deliverance, God used Moses to set the people free. Phenomenal.

Oh, that I had that kind of Crazy Faith.

PERSONAL APPLICATION
Here are a few questions to consider:

- Are there people who are holding me back from living in Crazy Faith? Moses had a few. Am I willing to trust God, despite the way things look?
- What excuses am I making to keep me from doing what God wants me to do?
- Moses had Aaron to encourage him and hold him accountable. Who do I have that is encouraging me to have Crazy Faith?

Surround yourself with friends who will help you live with Crazy Faith.

A friend loves at all times, and a brother is born for a time of adversity.
Proverbs 17:17

.

7

FAITH THAT'S CRAZY: *Bill Sammons*
*But **without faith it is impossible** to please him: for he that cometh to God must believe that he is, and that he is a rewarder of them that diligently seek him.*
-Hebrews 11:6

ONE OF THE guys I admire most is my friend, Bill Sammons. Bill makes his home in Delaware and has always been one of the most humble people I've ever met. This is his story.

MY BEST FRIEND Rick and I had a low-budget radio show. We were twelve years old, and his bedroom was our studio. We had no transmitter—or even real microphones—but we had a state-of-the-art, portable cassette-tape recorder and plenty of energy, creativity, and time. Those were the days.

Rick and I did "improv" before we knew what it was. We'd listen to Bill Cosby doing the voices of God and Noah on the record player, and then we'd make up our own sketches doing multiple voices. If we needed a little reverb, no problem. I'd put Rick's metal trashcan on my head, hold the recorder, and voila! Instant reverb. We learned that if you recorded with batteries that were almost dead and then played it back with new batteries, you could sound like a chipmunk. I didn't know it at the time, but God was preparing us for our future careers. Rick now pastors the largest church in our region, and I'm in my fortieth year of broadcasting.

I remember the first time we went to a real radio station. Rick and I were part of a singing group—a quartet—and were invited to appear on a local station to sing and do an interview. I was sixteen and mesmerized. I was in electronics heaven with turntables and cart machines and reel-to-reel tape players and VU meters dancing to the pulsing sounds coming from the studio speakers. I have no memory of what we sang or what we said, but I do remember thinking this was perhaps the coolest place I had ever been.

Four years later, I graduated from the local community college with a degree in Journalism and embarked on a career as news director at that very radio station. I made ninety dollars per week with no benefits, but I had a confident feeling that I was doing what I was made to do. As is common in the broadcast business, I'd move onward and upward to bigger and better radio and TV stations over the next several years, but there was a feeling inside I couldn't shake.

I wanted to program a Christian radio station in my hometown. Not like the ones I had heard before, with old preachers and organ music. I wanted to program a Christian radio station that sounded as good as the mainstream stations, with nothing but contemporary Christian music twenty-four hours a day. I could hear it in my head. Amy Grant. Andraé Crouch. Randy Matthews and Larry Norman. The artists would change over the years, but I played this radio station in my head and dreamed about one day providing Christian radio to my community.

Also bouncing around in my head was the fact that I was living paycheck to paycheck and driving a 1972 Gremlin. Radio stations were for millionaires, and I wasn't in the game. I eventually got married, had a couple of sons, and left broadcasting to work in marketing so I could better provide for my family.

But the dream wouldn't go away. I remember interviewing for a job once, and the interviewer asked me what I would be doing five years from now if I could do anything, and I said "operating my own Christian radio station." We both laughed knowingly. *Like that's going to happen.* Still, the dream wouldn't go away.

One day in the mid-1980s, I was reading our community newspaper, and an article caught my attention. It said the Federal Communications Commission (FCC) had allocated a new FM frequency to Milford, Delaware and they were accepting applications. The problem was the deadline was only a week away. The rest of that night, I argued with myself. This was from God! My chance to start a Christian radio station! Then I heard, "You don't have enough money! You don't know how to run a radio station!"

The next day, I tracked down a communications attorney and got the details. It would take about $7,000 to apply. I'd need to hire an engineer, find a place to put a 328-foot broadcast tower, and certify that I had access to the funds to build the radio station, *if* I was awarded the license. A quick budget for equipment, legal fees, land, studio, etc. put the budget at about $250,000. Which ... after paying the $7,000 application fee ... was $250,000 more than I had. We had been saving money to build a house, and when I asked my wife if we could spend the money on a radio station application instead, she didn't hesitate.

The next day, I found a tower site, hired the lawyer and an engineer, and we got the application filed before the deadline.

I shared my vision with my dad, and he suggested I talk to one of his friends to see if they would be interested in being a partner with me in the radio station venture. Sonny Reed graduated from high school with my father, and he was a very successful businessman. When I told him what I wanted to do and how much it would cost, he agreed to borrow the money against his home. When the FCC finally approved our application, we started the construction process.

But ... not so fast.

I quickly learned that not everybody in the community was as excited about our project as I was. At our first zoning hearing to get approval to build the 328-foot tower, I was surprised to see some of the neighbors had been rallied to protest our plans.

The group was led by Toms River, New Jersey-native Spyro Stamat. He had recently moved to the area and built a new home. Spyro was concerned our tower would devalue his property, and he convinced about thirty other people who lived within five miles of the site that it would devalue theirs too. At the hearing, we heard complaints that the tower would cause TV reception interference, that it would fall and impede fire trucks and ambulances, and that it would negatively impact an old farmhouse that might be eligible for National Historic Preservation status. They pulled out all the stops. And they were successful. I lost the zoning vote.

I was devastated. I was certain God had given me this dream, the resources, the opportunity. So what was going on? Had I made a mistake? Had God made one?

A couple of months later, I found another potential site for the tower. It was a few miles away from the original site, but still within the limited radius the FCC had given us. The site was an abandoned migrant labor camp. It was grown up with weeds and infested with snakes and who knows what else. When I suggested we buy it, Sonny thought I was crazy, but he agreed it was our best option.

We went back to the county for a new round of zoning hearings and were surprised to see that Spyro had rounded up the neighbors once again to oppose our new site. It was then I suspected there was something deeper going on than just the construction of a radio tower.

This time, the county narrowly approved our zoning request, and we were given the green light to put up the tower and build the studios. We went in and tore down a couple of the buildings on the site, including a large warehouse where Green Giant had once washed and packed string beans and lima beans. We left two of the buildings standing, with plans to turn one into our offices and studio and leave the other one for future growth. It was August of 1990.

The renovations were underway, and the studio building had a new roof and walls and we were starting the electrical work. A few weeks before, a friend and I had ripped the original roof off the studio building. The material was old and rippled, consisting of large sheets that overlapped at the seams. We threw it into large piles with plans to haul it to the landfill.

But before we could, two men with badges stopped by. They told me they were with the Delaware Department of Natural Resources and Environmental Control (DNREC) and had received an anonymous call that I was polluting the environment and mishandling asbestos. I showed them the roofing material we had removed, and they ordered me to have it tested at a private lab to determine what was in it.

The test came back positive for asbestos. I was arrested, fined, and we were ordered to rope off the property with caution tape and have the asbestos professionally removed. It set us back several weeks and cost $10,000.

Before all of the roofing materials had been hauled away, the DNREC compliance officers called me to say they had received another tip. This time, they were told I had been hiding the asbestos and burying it on our property. They came down, poked a rod into the ground where the tipster told them I had buried the asbestos, and sure enough ... they found several large pieces that had been buried.

It wasn't the first time we had unwanted visitors on our property. Our "No Trespassing" signs were disappearing, and I replaced them each time.

The next day, a Saturday, Sonny and I were at the property pulling electrical wires through the walls so the electrician could come in on Monday and start hooking up the outlets. By now, we had spent tens of thousands of dollars in legal fees that we hadn't anticipated because of the constant barrage of opposition on the local and federal level. They had been successful in delaying us from signing on to take advantage of the summer advertising season, and if we

were delayed any more we would likely miss the Christmas advertising season and be forced to launch the station with very little cash
in the dead of winter, when advertising dollars are scarce.

As we pulled the wires and talked about the asbestos being put in
a hole on our property, Sonny remembered a verse he'd read that
morning. He was reading through the One Year Bible, and Psalms
57:6 said, "...They dug a pit in my path—but they have fallen into it
themselves." Sonny told me he thought that verse was for us. He said
our enemies would be caught in their own trap.

I decided I should help facilitate that, so I told Sonny I was going
to stay behind that Saturday evening and stake out our property with
my camera. I figured photographic evidence would be the only way
the DNREC police would believe my story. Sonny left around 5:00
p.m. to get some dinner and head over to the Eagle's Nest Family
Campground—a campground operated by my family as a ministry—
for a gospel music concert. I grabbed a sandwich from a convenience
store, hid my pickup in the woods, and sat in the back of the studio
building with my camera, waiting to see if anybody showed up.

I had barely finished my sandwich when I heard Spyro out by the
road. He was calling my name. I got my camera ready and I waited.
The voice got closer, and I could tell he was now between the two
buildings on our property. When he got to the spot where our tower
now stands, I stepped out and snapped a picture of him. Since it was
dusk, the flash went off, and Spyro whirled around to see me
standing there with my camera. He called me a few names not appro-
priate for this book and dared me to take his picture again. So I did.

Next thing I knew, he head butted me, his forehead to the bridge
of my nose, and I went down in a heap. As I reached up to catch the
blood pouring out of my nose, Spyro ripped the camera out of my
hands, opened the back, and pulled out the film canister, exposing
the film to the light. He then smashed my camera against the cement-
block walls of the building and asked me where my witnesses
were now.

By then I had gotten back on my feet. I told Spyro that he was on
private property and he needed to leave. Instead, he swung his right

fist and punched me in the throat. I went down again like a sack of potatoes. I had never been in a fight in my life, and my odds in this one didn't look good.

As I lay on the ground, all the years of frustration and anger rushed out of Spyro, and he started screaming and kicking me in the head and back and shoulders. At various times, he told me that he heard voices telling him to kill me and that he was a demon. I wish I could say that I stood up and took spiritual authority over the obvious spiritual and physical attack that was happening to me, but it never crossed my mind. Instead, I let him hit me until he seemingly tired of not having me fight back. We both heard a friend of Spyro's out on the road yelling for Spyro to stop and to leave. Thankfully he did, but not before coming back to tell me that if I called the police he would kill my wife and sons. With the anger I had just witnessed, I didn't doubt his sincerity.

I drove myself back to the convenience store where I had bought a sandwich an hour before and called the campground, knowing my mom would answer the phone. I told her I had been beaten up. She knew who had assaulted me without asking. She told me to call the State Police and that she'd have dad come drive me to the hospital. I told her that I was afraid to call the police because of Spyro's threat, and she assured me she would take my wife and kids to a safe place and that I needed to call the police.

Spyro was arrested and charged with felony assault, trespassing, and a few other things. As part of sentencing, he was ordered to stay away from my family and me for one year. Even with the court order, my family was on edge. We lived in the woods, and any time a squirrel ran by the window, my wife jumped. My boys, who were four and seven at the time, would ask me questions about that night, and they associated bad people with the man who beat up their dad.

Less than three months after the assault, the radio station went on the air. It was November 5, 1990. We made it through the lean winter and were building an audience, and God was using this new radio station in ways I hadn't imagined. In the spring, we decided to host a concert, featuring some of our staff, at Eagle's Nest Family Campground. Our staff included several great singers, including two who had performed professionally prior to joining the station.

As we finished the sound checks and the audience started to trickle in with their lawn chairs and blankets, I had to do a double-take. Spyro was in the crowd with his wife and children. My dad saw him and asked whether we should call the police. This was an obvious violation of his probation, and we wondered if he was here to cause a disturbance during the concert. We decided to wait and see what he was up to.

A few minutes later, Spyro caught my eye and came up to me. I shook his hand and welcomed him, and he asked if he could meet with me, my Dad, and Sonny backstage after the concert. I told him, "Of course."

After the show, we gathered backstage to hear what he had to say, admittedly skeptical and cautious. What he said was the last thing we expected.

He started by apologizing for assaulting me and for everything that he had done to stop the radio station. He said he had secretly been listening to the station and had even called in once or twice under a false name to my dad's Saturday-morning talk show. He told us he had attended an Easter service at a local church and had accepted Jesus as his Savior. He said he didn't want to be my enemy any more. He wanted to be my friend. He then asked my dad, a pastor, if he would baptize him.

You could have knocked us over with a feather.

It was a modern-day Saul becoming Paul. My dad baptized him the following Sunday in front of a stunned congregation, and the story of his conversion even made the front page of Delaware's largest daily newspaper a few months later. The story was featured in *Guideposts* magazine. Most importantly, he did become my friend.

A couple of years later, a massive ice storm devastated our community. Many people were without power for weeks, and the radio station suffered damage to our roof from falling trees and ice from the antennas and tower. The first person to come by with a chainsaw and tarps to help was Spyro.

My friends asked me how I was able to stay focused and keep my faith during all the trials of getting the radio station started. Finances, legal battles, the environmental issues, zoning, getting assaulted and having my family threatened ... how did I keep going?

Honestly, I never thought about it. God had given me this crazy vision, and along with it, a big dose of Crazy Faith. I learned many things along the way—most importantly that God is more concerned about me than He is about my ministry. If we keep our eyes on God, our shoulder to the work He has called us to, and leave the details up to Him, He will deliver.

I used to read Psalm 37:4, where it says God will give us the desires of our heart. I thought it meant that whatever I wanted, God would give it to me. I wanted a radio station, so if I prayed hard enough, He would give it to me. Recently, I have come to learn that what the scripture really means is that if I draw close to God and seek His will, He will place the desires in my heart that He wants me to have. It won't look like we think it will. It won't happen as fast as we hope. But the final chapter, when written by God, is better than the one we could ever write.

8

THE GIFT OF LIFE
Abraham
I have come that you might have life, and have life more abundant.
-John 10:10

YOU READ the previous story about Bill Sammons, and the many sacrifices he made to step out and follow God with Crazy Faith are obvious. I've always been told that following God would require sacrifice. Over the last twenty years, I've experience it. The sacrifice of time, money, pleasure, convenience—it isn't foreign to me. And it's probably not foreign to you.

Every one of us knows about sacrifice at some level. Maybe as a young person who played a sport, you had to practice, practice, practice to improve your game. It required sacrifice. If you have kids or have ever worked with kids, you know the sacrifices involved in being a parent or child influencer. Sacrifice. If you have a job where you have worked to grow in your career or to be better at your craft, you know sacrifice. But the story of Abraham takes sacrifice to a whole different level. And it's really about more than sacrifice; it's about being obedient. Obedience with a level of faith that most of us would categorize as crazy.

Scriptures tell us that Abram (later Abraham) was a good man. He lived with his wife Sarai, but they had no kids. God came to Abram and said, *"Pack up your bags, I want you to leave home. I will show you the land, and I will make your family great; I will be with you and because of you all the families of the earth will be blessed"* (Genesis 12:1). With that promise, Abram packed up, trusted God, and headed out. He was seventy-five years old.

Then one night, God appeared to Abram and told him to look up at the sky. "You will have a son, he will have children, and his children will have children and they will be like the stars in the sky," God said.

At seventy-five, Abram wasn't so sure about this but he believed God, and his belief pleased the Lord. Perhaps our belief in what God says is the fuel that brings it to come to pass.

Abram decided he should share this encounter with his wife, Sarai. Her response? Laughter. Many years passed (Genesis 16) and Abram and Sarai still didn't have children. He must have been wondering. Sarai definitely was; she suggested that Abram have his child by their maidservant, Hagar. Unfortunately, Abram agreed.

When God promises to do something incredible that will yield incredible results, there will always be those that have a suggested shortcut for you to take.

Some of them will be well-meaning friends and possibly even family members. In our world of fast-food Christianity, where we can microwave and serve up anything lickity-split, we sometimes want that same shortcut to spiritual growth and spiritual fruit. God made a promise to Abram. And God will always honor His promise and fulfill it—His way and in His timing.

When Hagar became pregnant, trouble brewed between the maidservant and Sarai. Hagar ran away until she encountered God on her journey. He told her to go back and serve Sarai and Abram and that her son should be called Ishmael, which means, "God hears."

More years passed, and Sarai and Abram didn't have children.

The next time God appeared to Abram, Abram was ninety-nine years old. He reiterated His promise to him and said, "From now on your name will be Abraham, which means 'the God of many nations.' And your wife shall be called Sarah, which means 'princess.' I will bless her and she will have a son."

Sarah was ninety at this point. Abraham laughed and asked, "What about Ishmael? Can't my family come from him?"

"No," God said, "your wife will have a son. Call him Isaac, which means 'He laughed,' because you laughed when I told you."

Later, as Abraham sat by his tent, three men approached. He ran to greet them and offered them water. He and his wife, Sarah, prepared a meal for the guests. Abraham served the meal to them.

"Where is your wife?" one of them asked.

"She's inside the tent," Abraham answered.

"When we come back nine months from now, your wife will have a son," the stranger replied.

Sarah stood in the door of the tent and began to laugh. Nine months later, she had a son ... just as God promised.

It's important to know the birth story of Isaac so that when we read what God asked Abraham to do later, it's in context. Abraham and Sarah had prayed for a son, and God had provided. They loved their boy. But the next test was one they did not see coming. There was no foreshadowing of what Abraham would be asked to do.

One day, God called out to Abraham and asked him to take his son on a trip to a mountain, and on that mountain he would be required to offer Isaac as a burnt offering.

"What?" Abraham must have thought, "Did I hear you correctly?"

But Abraham followed God's instructions, loaded up wood and the donkey, and set out with two servants and Isaac on a three-day journey before they got to the place where God told them to stop.

"Wait here with the donkey while Isaac and I go worship God,"

Abraham told the servants. Then he placed the wood for the sacrifice on Isaac's back, and father and son headed up the mountain.

On the way up the mountain, Isaac asked about the animal for the sacrifice. Abraham told him that the Lord would provide. Once at the designated spot on the mountain, Abraham laid his son on the altar and prepared to sacrifice him.

Imagine what father and son were feeling. Can you picture the emotion? Was Abraham wondering where this provision of the Lord would come from? And Isaac? He's tied to the altar. Is he thinking that his father has totally lost it? I'm not sure of the conversation; the Bible doesn't record it for us. And I am glad.

Abraham was prepared to obey God, no matter what. But he also knew God has made a promise. Just like He made a promise to Moses. And God always keeps His promises. So Abraham was ready to kill his son, perhaps believing that even if Isaac died, God could raise him from the dead.

Just as he raised the knife, an angel of the Lord cried out, "Abraham, stop! Look! The Lord has provided a lamb for the sacrifice."

Can you imagine Isaac's thankfulness? He had to be thinking he was a goner.

And yet, God provided.

It's Crazy Faith that causes someone to be obedient like that. Where does that habit of obedience start? It starts in the small things.

I don't remember how old I was. I was probably seven or eight years old, and my mom and I were coming out of a store called K-Mart. My mom was fiddling with her keys and the bag of stuff she purchased, but in the other hand she was shaking the change. She had a puzzled look on her face. We arrived at the car, and I was hungry and ready to grab lunch from my favorite drive-thru.

She looked at me and said, "Jack, I have to go back in."

"Why?" I asked.

My mom explained that the lady at the register had given her back too much money.

I can't remember how much it was, but I don't even think it was more than a dollar. "Forget it and come on, Mom. I'm hungry."

"No, son, we have to go back in. I know in my heart that's what I need to do. She may get in trouble if her register comes up short, and it's the right thing to do."

I didn't think too much of it at that moment, but as we pulled away from the K-mart and headed to the fast-food restaurant, I knew my burger was going to taste better. My mom had done the right thing, and I knew it was the right thing. At that moment, my mom had listened to that still-small voice inside and been obedient. It wasn't convenient to go back into the store and return to the register, wait in line, and sort it all out, but *it was being obedient*. If we only do what is right and God-honoring when it's convenient or doesn't cost us anything, we will fall short of real integrity.

If we want to live with Crazy Faith, we have to learn the discipline of being obedient, even in the small things.

The path to Crazy Faith will be marked by times of testing from the Lord. I don't think God is testing us to see if He can trust us; He's all-knowing, so He already knows the answer to that. Perhaps His testing is to build our character and confidence in Him and in ourselves so we are more willing to step out in the realm of Crazy Faith.

PERSONAL APPLICATION
Here are a few questions for you to consider:

- What am I willing to sacrifice to follow God in Crazy Faith?
- Is there any area of my life that I have told God is off-limits?
- What area of my life do I feel like God is testing me in right now?

Ask God to give you the kind of Crazy Faith Abraham had.

Therefore, I urge you, brothers and sisters, in view of God's mercy, to offer your bodies as a living sacrifice, holy and pleasing to God—this is your true and proper worship.
Romans 12:1

9

STANDING ON THE WORD: *Kathy Nicholson*
For the word of God is alive and active. Sharper than any double-edged
sword, it penetrates even to dividing soul and spirit, joints and marrow; it
judges the thoughts and attitudes of the heart..
-Hebrews 4:12

AFTER READING the story of Abraham, we should be encouraged because God provided the lamb and spared Abraham's son. But what if the story had ended differently? What if God had not spared his son? He would have had to bring him back from the dead, since He promised that from him the nations would be blessed and more generations would come, right?

I wonder if, in our North-American mindset, we assume that if we put our full faith in Christ, everything turns out the way we want it. Do we think our definition of success and blessing is always the same as God's definition? What happens when God moves differently than we expect or hope? Does that make Him any less ... God? I think when God moves in a way we don't expect—maybe even in a way we hoped He would not—our response to *that* requires more faith, Crazy Faith. Let me give you a case in point of a friend I have watched demonstrate Crazy Faith in the last couple of years. Was it painful for her? Yes. Was it always easy? No. Were there tears? Was there anger? Has faith risen up in her to give her strength? Yes, yes, and *yes!* Her name is Kathy, and this is her story.

I HAVE BEEN in love with the Lord since I was thirteen years old, when I discovered He understood every single detail about me even when I didn't. As an accident-prone child with attention deficit problems and later diagnosed with dyslexia, people often misunderstood me. My oldest sister, Kim, had an elevated intelligence, and people marveled at this unique characteristic she possessed. My younger sister, Jenny, had the most beautiful brown eyes and the sweetest easy-going personality that people, including myself, found comforting. My younger brother, John—well, he was the baby of the family and the only boy. Need I say more?

Then there was Kathy: always challenging opinions, breaking the rules, and able to talk the horns off of a billy goat. No one ever came out and said I was a difficult child, but I could tell when people chose my siblings over me.

One day, in the midst of childhood, I had a change of direction. I discovered my leadership abilities. Instead of trying to be liked, I learned to lead. I discovered that children follow people who have cavalier ideas of greatness. I took an interest in singing, piano, and Scripture memorization, and all of these performance-driven abilities brought me the attention I craved.

At age thirteen, I had a life-altering experience with God. My heart was reborn for worship, and Jesus anointed my life for ministry. I spent the next years desperately seeking God's plan and purpose for my life. During my freshman year in college, I landed a job in radio.

Little did I know, God had created and gifted me to inspire people. A simple, exciting, new adventure would lead to a lifelong career as a radio personality, worship leader, and motivational speaker. One of the ways I have been able to lead people is by being a transparent person and sharing both the successes and failures of my life. The work of God's hands upon my life becomes even more evident with every intimate detail I share.

I went on to marry Dennis Nicholson in 1989, and we have three children: daughters Kara and Hannah and a son, Andrew. I was a stay-at-home mom until all my children started school. Even after they started school, I was blessed that my career worked around my family instead of my family working around my job. My first calling has always been to my family.

Mother's Day 2013 opened a new chapter of my life I will call "The Loss Factor." On her way back from working a 12-hour shift as a CNA, Kara lost control of the truck she was driving and crashed head-on into a tree. Kara's pelvis was shattered in the wreck, and she spent the next eighteen months struggling to walk. She eventually had nearly a dozen surgical procedures, including a complete hip replacement. The emotional strain this put on my faith was tremendous. There were many times during this trial I found myself barely hanging on. With every wave of struggle, I could feel myself going under. Each time I would cry out to Jesus, and He would rescue me.

Kara had the total hip replacement in March 2014. This was followed by a knee surgery a few months later. My youngest daughter, Hannah, was a true sister to Kara. Both were trained as CNAs, and Hannah knew how to help her sister better than I could in some ways. I will never forget watching Hannah shave Kara's legs and thinking to myself, *now that's the true love of a sister in action.*

In late May 2014, Hannah began complaining about a bump on her thigh. Hannah was a responsible young lady with a good job, so after work one day, she went to the emergency room at our local hospital to have it checked out. They gave her some antibiotics, and it seemed to clear up. A few weeks later, another bump showed up, and

Hannah again sought treatment at the ER. When another showed up and created a boil, Hannah took time off from work and went to see her primary physician. The bump was lanced, and more antibiotics were given.

The last week Hannah spent at home was the week of her birthday. Her daddy and I cooked exactly the meal she asked for: homemade mashed potatoes, Velveeta Shells and Cheese, a charcoal-grilled Rib-eye steak (her daddy's specialty), and a chocolate, sour cream pound cake. It would be the last full meal she would ever have.

The following week, Hannah became very ill. She went back to the doctor and then to the ER. This time they did an MRI. The discharge papers said she had a bulging disc and possibly a urinary tract infection. By Monday, she couldn't walk and was running a high fever. I decided to drive her to the emergency room at another hospital.

On the way to the hospital, she began to complain she couldn't breathe. The hospital immediately placed her into the intensive care unit and diagnosed her with MRSA, a staph infection that is antibiotic resistant. What we didn't know was that the MRSA had become septic in her blood and attacked her lungs. Within sixty-nine days, Hannah passed away from the damage done to her lungs. At the time of her death, she was on two forms of life support, waiting to be added to an organ-donor list so she could receive a double lung transplant.

During those long sixty-nine days, I was constantly by her side. It was the worst of times but still a precious gift to have her conscious part of the time and able to communicate with us. I was tempted to retreat into this dark place our family had been dragged, but I knew these were not just storm waves like I had faced during the wreck Kara had been through. These were hurricane—no—Tsunami-sized waves. My faith was undergoing the test of a lifetime.

I prayed for Hannah's healing, and I believed for it. I spoke Scriptures over her and I prayed the most sincere prayers I have ever prayed in my life. I knew there was no fooling God. I prayed that God would help me be real with Him and expose any hidden agenda I might have that would separate His presence from my or Hannah's life. God was with me and helping me not just to survive the storm but walk on the waves.

On Hannah's fifth day of hospitalization in the ICU, she was airlifted to Piedmont Hospital in Atlanta. Upon arriving at the hospital, as we were waiting for Hannah to be admitted and put into a room, we were sent to the waiting room. In the corner sat a baby grand piano. I have never been to a hospital with a piano in the waiting room, but God knew I would need this and that it would bless others too.

During the hardest of days, I would take a short break from Hannah's bedside to play the piano. The first time I played, I was oblivious to anyone else around me. I knew I had to get in touch with God or I would not have the strength to go on. Each time I played, I felt God's presence come into the room. People were touched by the obvious strength God downloaded as I struggled to worship Him during the worst storm of my life.

Another amazing realization manifested during this time. I had written seven songs the year before. As I began to sing them at the piano, I realized God had inspired these very songs to guide me through this life-altering time. Using my own words, God had prepared my heart in so many ways. I never once felt alone. I felt closer to God than I ever have before, and at times when I thought I was about to lose my balance, God was so close to me He simply leaned in and held me up. He did this supernaturally but also physically through the love and care of close family and friends—even strangers on several occasions.

I often prayed that God wouldn't take my daughter. "Please don't require this of me, Lord, but if You do, You will have to help me walk, because I don't think I can live in that world."

God did require it of me, and for whatever reason—which I still do not know—Hannah went to be with Jesus on October 19, 2014. She was surrounded that day by her family, including: me, her daddy, brother, sister, husband, her grandmother, and her aunts, uncles, and cousins. More than twenty minutes before they told us she was gone, the presence of God rested upon me, and I knew she was leaving us. I told my husband and family.

It was the supernatural peace of God that brought any manifestation of comfort to our family in those early hours of tragic loss. In the days to come, God continued to lead me with supernatural strength.

Most every single day Hannah was sick, I posted updates to Facebook. There was a growing interest in Hannah's story as the days passed. Hundreds of thousands of people were praying for us. In the days immediately preceding Hannah's passing, Fox News in Atlanta featured Hannah's plight for a lung transplant. Other Fox News stations across the nation picked up the story. Fox News honored Hannah's life with a priceless tribute when she passed away a few days later. The words of those who knew and loved Hannah were broadcast to millions, and a faith in God beyond death was witnessed to the world.

In the months since we last said our goodbyes to Hannah on this side of heaven, a foundation called Hannah's Hope has been created to assist others in the awareness, prevention, and treatment of MRSA. Hannah Nicholson no longer needs hope; she is with the God of all hope. My heart is to pass on her hope to others.

In addition, I see a great need to impact the organ-donor process so others will not be left like Hannah was, waiting to be added to a donor list. When the legislative session began in 2015, our Georgia State Representative Terry Rogers introduced a bill in Hannah's honor that would greatly increase the likelihood of organ donors in the state of Georgia. On March 2, 2015, the House unanimously approved the bill. We are now waiting for the State Senate to vote on the bill. We believe it will soon be law and only the beginning of the work that Hannah's Hope will bring others.

$\sim$

KATHY'S CRAZY Faith is making a difference. She is taking what has been a hard road to travel and using what she learned in the process to help others, both physically with MRSA and spiritually, as she shares the light of Christ with those she comes in contact with. That's Crazy Faith.

10

THE GOD I KNOW: *Daniel*

...that I may know Him and the power of His resurrection and the
fellowship of His sufferings, being conformed to His death;
-Philippians 3:10

The book of Daniel opens in 605 BC while Jehoiakim, the eldest son of Josiah, had been made king of Judah. Jehoiakim had wasted state funds on a new residence for himself (Jeremiah 22:13-19) and destroyed Jeremiah's writings of Jehoiakim's own impending doom.

Sent by his dad, King Nebuchadnezzar, the soon-to-be-king of Babylon had come to Jerusalem to seize the city and was to lead the Babylonians to defeat Egypt.

Daniel, a teenager, was about to be thrown headlong into this whirlwind of activity. It was a crazy time.

King Nebuchadnezzar called out to one of his officials, a young guy named Ashpenaz, and told him to find some young men for his service amongst the sons of Israel. His qualifications were many: The young men must have no defect. They must be good-looking. They must be intelligent in every area. They must have common sense and knowledge. They must have abilities the king could use.

His objective? To find these young men and enlist them in a three-year training period to teach them the literature and culture of the Chaldeans, including math, astronomy, and agriculture. Then he'd enlist them into his personal service.

Among those chosen were Daniel, Hananiah, Mishael, and Azariah. But the commander of the officials gave them pagan names after the heathen gods. The original names for Daniel (God is judge), Hananiah (Yahweh is gracious), Mishael (Who is what God is), and Azariah (Whom Yahweh helps) were changed to Belteshazzar (May Bel protect his life), Shadrach (the moon god), Meshach (Who is what Aku is?) and Abed-nego (Servant of Nebo). We soon discover, however, that changing their names or what they were called didn't change who they were. They were to be young men who demonstrated Crazy Faith.

Isn't it interesting how the world has changed the names of many things to try to make them something different? Some call pro-life "anti-abortion." If we stand for marriage between one man and one woman, we're "anti-gay." The bottom line is this: changing what you call it doesn't change what it is.

So what did Daniel do? Daniel stepped out in Crazy Faith.

Stepping out in Crazy Faith will always lead you against the status quo.

DURING THE YOUNG men's training time, they were to eat only the king's choice food and drink. Those were the king's orders. There were to be no exceptions.

Daniel "made up his mind" (Daniel 1:8) that he would not defile himself with the king's food. Daniel knew that the food had not been killed in accordance with Mosaic Law and, furthermore, had been offered up to a pagan god. He was determined that he would honor God with his life, despite the situation. He was prepared to tell the officials and the king that he would not be eating the king's food, even though the king had commanded it.

Surely he knew the king would have him killed. He would be deliberately disobeying the king's order, purposefully going against the commands of the culture. Yet he still held to his Crazy Faith.

How did he do it? Scriptures tell us that he was *determined*. Determination: How much you will give or give up in a situation to remain resolute and on course.

To exercise Crazy Faith, you will have to be determined.

DANIEL ASKED one of the commanders if he could abstain from eating the food. Instead of abstaining, throwing out the food, or hiding it, he asked the commander directly. That Daniel would try to honor the commander and do the will of God at the same time displays how deeply he trusted God. His wisdom also gave Daniel an umbrella of protection, because the commander was a buffer between him and the king.

Why would Daniel do this? The king was the authority of the land, even though he was incorrect in his leadership. Daniel wanted to honor the authority of the land and honor God. That kind of attitude is what moves faith into the realm of craziness. Would that make a difference in the commander's decision? Maybe. Maybe not. So why was Daniel bold enough to demonstrate such amazing faith? Maybe Daniel knew if he took the path of honor, the glory God would receive would be even bigger.

Many years ago, a friend of mine named Foster served as a student pastor. One night, he received a knock on his apartment door from a young lady named Sarah, who lived above him. Sarah was the daughter of two of his seminary friends. He opened the door and saw her sullen face. "Sarah, so good to see you. What can I do for you?"

"I need your advice."

"Come, have a seat." Foster led her to the couch and motioned for her to sit. "Advice about what, sweetie?"

She sighed. "I'm on the cheerleading squad at school, and the cheer we're supposed to do this weekend has some suggestive moves I'm not comfortable performing. I don't know what to do. I don't want people to make fun of me, but I don't want to participate. Can you help me figure it out?"

Foster was blown away that this fourteen-year-old girl had that kind of sensitivity to God and such an innocent heart. "Sarah, I can tell you what to do, but instead of me making the decision for you, I want you to pray about it and do what you feel God is leading you to do."

Sarah agreed. They prayed together, asking God to speak clearly and for Sarah to have a listening heart. Then Sarah left.

The following Saturday, there was a knock at his door. Sarah was back holding a VHS tape and said, "Do you want to watch the cheerleading routine we did last night?"

Foster was intrigued. "Sure!"

Sarah slid the videotape into the machine and hit the play button. The cheerleading team filled the screen and the routine began.

Foster told me that he watched as the cheerleading squad did their first routine. Sarah performed and did a fabulous job. When the music ended, the girls got ready for the second routine. As the music began, Sarah skipped off the court and took a seat on one of the bleachers. The routine continued with some vulgar and inappropriate movements and applause from those in the stands. When the routine ended, Sarah stood up, joined her teammates center court, and then exited with them.

"Wow," Foster said. "I'm speechless! And so proud of you for holding to your convictions!"

Sarah went on to tell Foster she had prayed about it, felt God leading her in her decision, and then approached the cheerleading sponsor. Sarah shared her convictions and had been given permission to sit out for that routine. Fourteen-year-old Sarah honored her teacher and honored God, even while the crowd in attendance gave thunderous applause for a routine she found inappropriate. Someone standing up for her convictions and following the leadership of God when every other voice is shouting to go in the opposite direction is rarely seen today. That's Crazy Faith.

What was the result of Daniel's conviction not to defile himself with the king's food? God intervened and gave Daniel favor and compassion with the commander. When Daniel shared his conviction with the commander, no doubt the man was concerned about losing his head to the king if he was found out, especially if Daniel and his friends looked less healthy than the others who had eaten the king's food.

When the commander expressed his concern, Daniel made a suggestion. He asked the commander for ten days to eat only vegetables and water and prove that he and his friends would look healthier than the others. Part of having Crazy Faith is not just determination. It's *dedication*. Dedication: How long will you remain resolute and on course to accomplish the task?

At the end of the ten days, Daniel and his friends passed the test. They continued to eat only the vegetables and water ... for the remaining three years. Did you see that? Their dedication to the task of honoring their Lord and denying themselves the king's food was *three years*. That's true dedication. We often think of dedication in short term, but real dedication by definition implies longevity—a long-term commitment to a goal.

The result of Daniel's and his friends' dedication and determination was favor from the king. They were able to gain tremendous knowledge during their three-year crash course. But Daniel gained something even more valuable than knowledge. He gained the wisdom needed to understand visions and dreams.

Knowledge comes from human reasoning, learning, and growth. It's highly valued. More than ever, it's needed in our world. In this day and age, a college degree is almost imperative if one wants to be successful. Education has always been important.

Wisdom comes from God. It's the ability to "connect the dots" with the knowledge that we have gained. "Knowledge is the ability," someone once said, "to take an engine apart. Wisdom is the ability to put it back together." Wisdom also comes only from longevity. People who have wisdom have invested the time necessary to acquire it. It doesn't come easy; it comes from dedication. And that's why Daniel received it.

Daniel and his friends were presented to the king, and out of all the other young men, only Daniel, Hananiah, Mishael, and Azariah were found fit for the king's personal service. Daniel 1:19 says, "...so they entered the king's personal service." Not only that, but the last verses say Daniel and his friends were ten times better in wisdom and understanding than all the others. God honored Daniel's and his friends' determination and dedication.

PERSONAL APPLICATION

Here are a few questions to consider:

- How does this concept apply to me now?
- How determined am I to follow the Lord's commands for my life?
- What temptations am I willing to forego in order to honor the Lord?
- What am I willing to give up, to risk, in order to do the thing God has called me to do?
- Am I ready to demonstrate Crazy Faith?
- Is there a limit to the lengths I will go to in order to serve Him?
- How dedicated am I in my discipleship?
- Am I weary in my well doing?

Stay determined and dedicated. Your destination is the service of the King.

Let us not become weary in doing good,
for at the proper time we will reap a harvest if we do not give up.
– Galatians 6:9

11

LOVE DEMONSTRATED
Jack and Christina Cleland
This is how God showed his love among us: He sent his one and only Son
into the world that we might live through him.
-I John 4:9

The story of Daniel reminds me of Jack and Christina Cleland, two friends who demonstrated dedication and determination in the midst of a major life trial. I vividly remember standing in the hospital waiting room with a lot of friends and family members. We were all anxious to hear the news about Jack and Christina's little baby girl. Many people were talking and some were praying. Others were trying to be distracted by watching television, but the local program was interrupted.

Scenes from New York City appeared on the screen as reporters tried to explain how an airplane flew into one of the World Trade Center towers. Smoke and fire billowed out of a gaping hole in the side of one of the towers, and we all looked on with horror and disbelief. Meanwhile, Jack and Christina were in the midst of their own drama.

Several months earlier, Jack and Christina, discovered they were having their first child.

~

WITH EXCITEMENT IN OUR HEARTS, my wife Christina and I headed to the doctor for Christina's appointment. This was the day we were going to find out if our baby was a boy or a girl. We were ready to start a family, and things looked great.

We entered the doctor's office and went into the room for the ultrasound. The technician showed us our baby's arms, legs, and heart and explained what we were seeing on the screen and then excused herself. Christina and I discussed baby names as we waited for the doctor to enter.

The doctor entered the room and sat down and began with some very peculiar questions. He then went on to say, "Your baby has a condition where its bones are not going to grow to keep up with the rest of the body. At birth, the baby will not be able to breathe and will probably suffocate within a few minutes."

Silence. The words slowly penetrated our hearts. Christina cried while I desperately tried to find words to console my best friend and soul mate. Utter disbelief echoed in our minds.

The doctor laid out our choices. "You have three options. Terminate the pregnancy, carry the baby to term and let nature take its course, or get a second opinion."

Each choice was like a dagger in our hearts. None of them sounded acceptable. This child was a gift from God, and life was important no matter the outcome.

After a moment, the doctor asked, "Would you like to know the sex of the baby?"

We looked at each other and nodded.

"You're having a baby girl."

The walk to the car seemed like it took forever. Once inside, all we could do was hold each other and sob. We felt paralyzed. *What do we do? Where do we go? Who can we talk to?* As we contemplated what to do, only one thing came to mind—pray. But we wanted to pray for our baby girl by name. The gift of this child was a gift of grace, so that would be her name.

Grace.

The following week, we went in for a second opinion on Grace's condition. The first diagnosis was verified. The condition that Grace had made it unable for a child to sustain respiration on her own. As long as Grace was being carried by Christina, she would be alive, free to move and kick. However, as soon as she entered the world and needed to breathe on her own, she would suffocate.

Over the next several weeks, as follow-up ultrasounds continued to confirm the inevitable, another problem was developing. One of the side effects of Grace's condition was extra amniotic fluid. This extra fluid would lead to a larger-than-normal amniotic sack which could potentially cause a uterine rupture, a life threatening complication for Christina. Inducing labor at thirty-five weeks seemed to be the best option. The emotional struggle was the realization that we were having to schedule the last day on earth with Grace. A parent burying their child is not normal, and we knew it would require some Crazy Faith. The prayer was that God would step in and call Grace home in his timing. Days later, early one morning, the prayer was answered. Christina went into labor.

As our lives changed forever and we delivered Grace, our country experienced something horrific. Grace was beautiful with a perfect little face and head full of hair, so peaceful. At the same time, the World Trade Centers were beginning to fall. As the world stood still, we held Grace, gave her a bath, and dedicated her to the Lord.

THIS COUPLE'S journey inspires me for many reasons.

For those close to Jack and Christina, we know the Crazy Faith they both exemplified on their journey. The steadfast commitment they had to one another and to God, despite the probability of baby Grace's future, was unmistakable. The story did not turn out like they wanted. It didn't turn out like *I* had hoped. And yet, God is still God and His strength and love for them was still constant all the way through their pregnancy and loss. Furthermore, God used their journey to make incredible impacts on the lives of people around them. Christina and Jack's model of faith spoke volumes to hospital staff and family members.

They wanted Grace's life to be counted and used for Christ. Jack's prayer was that God would use her in a mighty way, that someone at the funeral would accept Christ, and that the day of the funeral would be a beautiful day. Jack's prayers were answered. Two people came to Christ as a result.

The months following Grace's death were lonely and difficult for Jack and Christina. But they pressed on and continued to trust the Lord. God had a plan and they wanted to be ready. Unknowing to Christina, Jack began to pray for twins. He wanted friends and family to see God truly was good even when we don't understand why things happen the way they do. I am happy to say, God answered that prayer!

As they continued to seek direction for the calling God had placed in their life, Jack began praying. He had served as a high school teacher and youth minister. He wanted to make a difference in the lives of children and families. As time passed, it became clear to him that he could have a ministry he had never seen or considered before; a ministry in the medical field. Fast forward to 2015. Dr. Jack Cleland is now a pediatrician in Spartanburg, South Carolina. He and Christina have three boys.

There's a passage in the book of Daniel where Daniel and his friends are about to be thrown into the fiery furnace for failing to bow to the king. They see the fire, they know it's hot, and they know what selling out will mean to their souls. So, they commit to be steadfast in their faith, trusting their God while not knowing the outcome. We know the Lord rescued them from the fire, but they didn't know that was going to happen. I know they were glad that they were rescued, but frankly, it doesn't change their level of commitment and the Crazy Faith they exhibited. When I think of Jack and Christina, I think about that story, and I think about what those young guys said to the king.

"*Hear, o hear us, O King, we will not bow down and worship the idol you have set up because we worship the One True God. So throw us in the fire if you must and our God will rescue us. But even if He does not rescue us, we will not bow down*" (Daniel 3:18).

Totally committed. All in. Sold out. Crazy Faith.

12

SEND SOME RAIN

Noah

"You heavens above, rain down my righteousness; let the clouds shower it down. Let the earth open wide, let salvation spring up, let righteousness flourish with it; I, the LORD, have created it.."

-Isaiah 45:8

J ack and Christina remained committed, despite the way things looked. That seems to be a theme when it comes to having Crazy Faith. The Scriptures tell us that we *"walk by faith, not by sight"* (2 Corinthians 5:7). That's hard to do, isn't it? But there's a reason the Scriptures tell us to do that. Sometimes things aren't what they seem.

How often have you or I made a decision based on sight, only to be disappointed? Maybe it was a food selection we made because it looked delicious or a job situation where the pay looked better. And, once we made the decision, we regretted it. Eve made her decision to eat the forbidden fruit of the Garden of Eden with the same criteria. (See Genesis 3:6.)

Making decisions based on the way things look will sometimes come back to bite us.

A great example of appearances not being what they are is the story of Noah. Noah was a God-fearing man. The people of the land had become idolaters, and God had given them more than enough chances to return to Him. (See Genesis 6:5.) But they had refused. They had gradually become more and more depraved, and no one would change their evil ways, despite many warnings from God. Everyone thought only of himself. They had no respect for others. Violence and sin were the norm. Sound familiar?

God told Noah that He was going to destroy the earth by a flood and that Noah should prepare to save himself and his family by building an ark. Flood? What's that? Noah had never seen rain. Raining so much that the earth is covered in water? Ark? What's an ark?

God's purpose wasn't to destroy the people, but to destroy wickedness and sin. He gave them one last chance. The 120 years it took Moses to complete the ark served as a period of grace for people to change their ways and repent.

Needless to say, Noah was hard pressed to believe what God was saying. He had no idea what was in store for him and his family. But God gave Noah very specific instructions as to how to build the ark. After all, he had never done this before!

When God asks you to step out in crazy faith, he will give you the instructions on what steps to take.

The ark was to be 300 cubits in length, fifty cubits in width, and thirty in height. It was to be three stories, divided into small rooms. As Noah prepared to build the ark that God had described and instructed, the people around him couldn't fathom the task. God told Noah to tell the people what he was building and to tell everyone its purpose: that it would save him from the coming Flood. They thought he was crazy. And they made fun of him. Yet, night and day he built. Even though there was no sign of rain to come.

When God asks you to step out in crazy faith, you may get made fun of, and people may think you're crazy.

Nearly twenty years ago, God led me to add a radio show to our non-profit ministry. The show was aimed at teenagers and aired on a local station where I grew up. It had a profound impact on my life as a teenager. In fact, I would say, it kept me from forsaking my faith and walking away from being a Christ-follower.

I remember going to some people and sharing about the idea of taking this local show to a national audience.

"Radio? You don't know anything about radio," some of them said.

"That's a stupid idea," others chimed in.

After several months of prayer and sharing the idea with my wife, I approached the host of the show, who also happened to be a close friend. Britt was open to the idea and invited me to research what it would take to do it. At that point in time, the only thing our ministry was involved in was camp ministry, and I would speak at student events around the country. We had a small staff and a small budget.

I began to investigate what it would take to syndicate this local show. Satellite time, marketing, promotion, and eventually adding staff were criteria the people I talked to said would be a requirement. The price tag was close to $100,000 for a one-year commitment.

Some of the same people I had talked to earlier began to ask questions about my research. "What have you found out?"

"Well, it's going to cost $25,000 just for the satellite time," I shared.

"Yep, thought it would be way too costly," he replied with a chuckle.

In my heart, I knew God was calling me to this task. And one by one, God gave me instructions and opened doors for me to walk through. Within a few months, God led me to a satellite delivery agency for radio broadcasters and individuals who stepped up to pay the initial satellite bill.

In March 1997, our radio show launched on twelve stations in various cities across the country, and by the next year, we were on over fifty stations. Parents began to support our ministry and our radio show from all over the country and help pay the bill for this ministry to teens. Out of the radio show, a television show was launched in 2000. It, too, became nationally syndicated within a year. Our radio show ran nationally for over fifteen years and was on over 250 radio outlets at its culmination. Countless lives were encouraged. Many young people came to faith in Christ, and all these years later, I still run into people who were affected by *The Sound of Light* radio show.

I sometimes look back and think about those people who laughed and thought I was crazy. But God had the last laugh. People laughed at Noah, too. But he didn't let that stop him from what God had called him to do.

The flood came. The waters rose. And Noah's family and the animals inside survived the flood and the storm. They lived in the boat for almost a year. And then the ground was dry again.

Crazy faith may require enduring some storms along the way.

Can you imagine being tossed upon the ocean for almost a year? Noah and his family endured the waters outside the boat. The result of their obedience took them on this journey. Sometimes, it's easy to believe that if we do what God wants us to do, everything will be a bed of roses. But the story of Noah shows that there may be storms for a season. Yet, as we learn from Noah, when the storms are over, God is there as He promises to be.

PERSONAL APPLICATION
Here are a few questions to consider:

- Who is making fun of you when you are trying to do something God has required of you?
- Are you following God's specific instructions?
- What are those instructions?
- Have you encountered storms during the process?
- Who are you leaning on during the storms?

Follow the instructions that God has given you on the journey of crazy faith.

Thy Word is a lamp unto my feet, and a light unto my path...
Psalm 119:105

13

DREAMING
John Waller
O God did I hear You?
You really want me to
Walk up to that mountain
Tell it just to move
This is crazy yeah

I had the privilege of meeting John Waller when he was in the music group According to John. I produced a syndicated radio show that aired across the country, and John's band was one of the artists that we played from time to time. They stopped by while coming through our area for an interview, and we got to hang out for a bit. Two things struck me about John: his heart and his humility. Fast-forward fifteen years and some things stay the same. John's heart and humility are two of them.Since I had seen John last, he had gone out as a solo artist for a few years and then moved to Colorado to lead worship. It was during his time in Colorado that God continued to refine his craft and give him songs that would connect with listeners around the world. One of the songs would be "While I'm Waiting."

Millions of people have heard it on radio or while watching the film *Fireproof*. The message in "While I'm Waiting" continues to inspire people around the globe and still causes people to e-mail John their stories of "waiting" on God. Little did John know, that song would also network him into relationship with many people that would help further his ministry.

MY WIFE JOSEE and I have always loved children and wanted to help our five children grow up learning to love God with a faith that was solid and a relationship that was true. From my total surrender as an eleventh-grade high school student to an artist, husband, and dad, I desired to follow after God with Crazy Faith. My heart for ministry came from that same desire.

Every believer is called to ministry. That's why I felt called. That's why I write songs. My gifting is to bring encouragement and truth through music.

As I followed God's desire for my life and the life of my family, God began to tug on Josee's and my hearts about the idea of adoption. Adoption had always been a part of my life; three of my cousins are adopted. Throughout our marriage, adoption had often been a topic of conversation. Finally, after spending time with several families who had adopted children from different parts of the world, we decided to think more seriously about it.

Adoption is highly contagious, and Josee caught the virus from seeing a little Chinese girl. It's the best kind of virus there is, because it helps us to understand the heart of God—maybe more than anything. That's what God has done for us; he's adopted us. We initially set out to adopt a little girl from China, but a dream changed everything. One night, after we'd been praying and fasting about our forthcoming adoption journey, I had a dream. In the dream, I was surrounded by older kids between middle- and high-school aged in an orphanage. They swarmed around, wanting to meet me. I caught a glimpse of a little girl out of the corner of my eye. She had long, straight, brown hair. She was no doubt a shy, loner type and looked to be about seven years of age. I studied her and then asked, "What's your name?"

She looked and me and said, "Anna."

"How old are you, Anna?"

"I'm ten," she replied.

As I stared in disbelief, I thought, *That's my daughter!*

My mom, who had passed away the day after my fifth child, Josiah, was born, then appeared in the dream. She was the first person that I told about Anna.

I woke up from the dream weeping and told Josee all about Anna. We knew that our daughter was somewhere in the world and we simply had to find her. God went on to confirm Anna's name more than five times over the next few days.

A few days later, Josee and I were sharing about our call to adoption with some friends. These friends had been working with Project 143. Project 143 is an Orphan Hosting Program. Hosting is inviting an orphan child to live in your home and experience your family for four to eight weeks over the summer or winter holiday. Host families have the opportunity to share their values, beliefs, and culture, as well as learn something new from their host child. Hosting is ideal for families with a heart for the millions of orphans worldwide. We fit that qualification to a tee. We also knew that without hosting, most of these children would eventually "age out" of the system and never experience the life-giving, life-changing love being in a family provides. When we got connected with P-143, we immediately asked if there were any girls in the hosting program that fit Anna's description, but we didn't mention her name. Her name was quickly confirmed one last time when a picture of one of the last girls waiting to be hosted was brought to our attention.

We opened the e-mail attachment with the photo of the girl. It was Anna. I said, "That's the girl in my dream!"

The young girl we were looking for was living in an orphanage in the Ukraine. Shortly after, we found out that Anna had a fourteen-year-old brother named Max, which really scared us. So much so that we almost backed away. But after praying and trusting in the peace that passes all understanding, we decided to bring Anna and her brother to stay in the Waller home for the summer.At the end of the hosting period, Anna and Max had to return to the Ukraine, but Josee and I were already way down the paper trail to adopt these wonderful children. Because of the ages of Anna and Max, it was relatively a quicker process than some adoptions. Within two months, our family had been given a November travel date to go to the Ukraine and complete the adoption.

I had already purchased the plane tickets, and we were so excited to travel to the Ukraine for a month or more. God provided all the finances we needed for the adoption, and to top it off, He provided so that all our children could accompany us.

We were still a month away from traveling when we received an e-mail informing us the following:

John and Josee,

I'm not sure how we missed this, but ... it appears Max and Anna have a twelve-year-old sister. She was sent to a separate orphanage due to an issue with her vision. If you're willing to take her too, I won't charge you any more money. Let me know how you would like to proceed.

Sincerely, Konstantine

We were shocked! "God, You wouldn't do that to us, would You?"

After the shock wore off, we came together as a family and prayed and discussed the opportunity we faced. Josee and I knew we could change a girl's destiny forever. We decided, by faith—sight unseen—to adopt this girl that we had never met. The siblings had been separated for seven years, and we were going to bring these kids back together, by faith. The entire time we were going through this process, the one thing we kept saying over and over was "This is crazy!"

I kept telling the Lord, "There better be a great song in all of this!" God came through on that one.

It's gonna take crazy faith,
So what if it costs me everything,

I'm stepping out,
I'm taking the leap of crazy faith.

If I said everything was perfect since our adoption, I would be lying. These kids, as all orphans, came with their own set of issues; there's baggage, without a doubt. They were rejected at a young age. At times, it's hard for them to receive love, so we are learning as we go.

THAT'S CRAZY FAITH. John would admit they don't have it figured out. But who does? To take it one day at a time and learn as we go—isn't that the way Jesus wants it? Doesn't that cause us to trust Him instead of trusting ourselves? Doesn't it also cause us to reach out to community to help us do what God has called us to do?

Crazy Faith will always cause us to rely on community, the body of Christ.

"We have great communities who stand around us, help us, sharpen us, and teach us about things that we don't know about when it comes to helping these kids navigate their way into our families," John shares. What about the lessons that have been learned when stepping out in Crazy Faith?"One of the greatest lessons I have learned through this Crazy Faith and adoption and being a father to six biological kids and three adopted is that they are equally mine. I'm as much the father of my adoptive kids as I am of my biological kids. And that's the same way we are in our relationship with our Heavenly Father who has adopted us," John says. "We believe in living a life of faith."

PERSONAL APPLICATION

- What crazy thing has God called you to step out and do?
- Are you ready?
- What if it costs you everything?

Take a leap ... of Crazy Faith.

But when he asks, he must believe and not doubt, because he who doubts is like a wave of the sea, blown and tossed by the wind. James 1:6

ACKNOWLEDGMENTS

There are a lot of people who made this book happen. I specifically want to thank a few:

I want to thank my family for their patience with me during this "crazy" process; I love them.

Thanks to The Gathering and my extended church family who have inspired me to live with Crazy Faith.

Big thanks to my ministry friends who I am privileged to serve at The Heart Share Group and supported this endeavor.

Special thanks to those modern day "crazy" people who shared their story in this book, so others could be inspired to take the leap.

Thanks to Alycia Morales for editing and Adam Hall for his creative input.

I would be remiss not to thank John Waller for the "Crazy Faith" song that inspired this idea; thanks for your partnership and friendship and demonstration of Crazy Faith.

AFTERWORD

CONTACT INFORMATION

Mike and Terica Williams: *www.cupsmission.com*
    If you'd like to go on a trip and serve the people of the Dominican Republic, check out www.cupsmission.com

Shelley Armato's E-mail:
    shelley.armato@mysmartplans.com

Bill Sammons: *www.887thebridge.com*
    E-mail: *bill@887thebridge.com*

Kathy Nicholson: *www.kathynicholson.com*

John Waller: www.johnwaller.org, visit i-Tunes to download his music.

ABOUT THE AUTHOR

Jack Eason is the Executive Director of the Crossover Cups Mission, a mission in the Dominican Republic helping young girls learn how to sew and sharing the gospel. Jack travels and speaks quite a bit around the country for conferences and non-profits.

To hear about the Crossover Cups Mission, subscribe to the podcast through Apple Podcasts by looking for "Crossover Cups Mission" or click the link at www.cupsmission.com .

Jack, his wife Lynette, an accomplished Christian Fiction author, and their two kids make their home in Greenville, SC.

Jack is available to come speak for your ministry event; just get in touch with his office.

www.jackeason.com
   www.cupsmission.com
   www.theheartsharegroup.com

Made in the USA
Lexington, KY
04 November 2019

56494873R00063